To Riu ♡

Love,

Kay

2026

My Name is Ken and I Will be Your Waiter for a Long, Long Time...

The life and faith of Kenneth E. Untener, bishop of the Diocese of Saginaw, Michigan, told in his own words

Based on the homilies, talks, and writings
of Kenneth E. Untener,
Bishop of Saginaw (1980-2004)

My Name is Ken and I Will be Your Waiter for a Long, Long Time...

The life and faith of Kenneth E. Untener, bishop of the Diocese of Saginaw, Michigan, told in his own words

Based on the homilies, talks, and writings
of Kenneth E. Untener,
Bishop of Saginaw (1980-2004)

Edited by Catherine Haven

Published by *Little Books* of the Diocese of Saginaw

ISBN 978-0-9863344-0-5

Published by *Little Books* of the Diocese of Saginaw
P.O. Box 6009
Saginaw, Michigan 48608-6653

www.littlebooks.org

Printed and bound
in the United States of America

Contents

Foreword

"My name is Ken and I will be your waiter for a long, long time . . ."

That's how Ken Untener introduced himself to the more than 6,000 people who attended his ordination as bishop of the Catholic Diocese of Saginaw, Michigan, on November 24, 1980.

He had been named the fourth bishop of this mid-Michigan diocese only six weeks earlier on October 4, 1980. Coming to Saginaw from Detroit (which was only hours away), he was already a familiar face for many people in the diocese. He had been rector of St. John's Provincial Seminary in Plymouth, Michigan, which had provided the theological education of most of the younger priests throughout the state, including the priests in Saginaw. He frequently visited Saginaw to see his sister and her family, and had given talks and retreats to the diocesan clergy.

Ken would serve the Saginaw diocese for nearly 25 years until his death on March 27, 2004.

Ken hadn't aspired to become a bishop. He frequently quoted his friend Richard Sklba, auxiliary bishop of the Archdiocese of Milwaukee, Wisconsin: "We are born into a time not of our choosing and given a task not always to our liking. And we will find God there or not at all, *for God is nowhere else.*" Ken believed that a priest's happiest day comes when he finally receives his first assignment as a pastor of a parish, and it was a role he had looked forward to one day.

When Cardinal John Dearden of the Detroit Archdiocese delivered the news that Ken was to head the Saginaw diocese, Ken suggested the name of another bishop to take his place. Cardinal Dearden told him he wasn't asking his opinion. Ken agreed to accept the post.

The new bishop-elect chose as his motto: "That They May Have Life," and promised to commit himself to that purpose. In a 2003 interview with the diocesan newspaper, *The Catholic Weekly*, Ken compared his role as bishop to that of a bridge-builder, rather than a rebel.

"I don't have to wrestle the demon because the rebel isn't in me," he explained. "I am a thinker, however, and I always ask three questions: Is this true? Am I the person to say it? Is it truth and love (because truth without love is not good and love without truth is weak)? If the answer to all three is 'yes,' then I do it."

Acknowledgements

The purpose of this book is to let Ken Untener tell the story of his vocation, priesthood, and ministry in his own words. And (ever the teacher), he often used stories of his life as a way to deliver a message from the Scripture and the strength of his faith.

This book is not a memoir. Ken did a lot of preaching and rarely used a prepared text, but often recorded his homilies and talks on a microcassette recorder tucked in his pocket. He spoke from his heart and he used examples from everyday life, sometimes even using an incident that had just happened to him that day.

Most of this book's passages come from homilies and talks that Ken delivered over the years. They are selections that people who knew Ken Untener found to be particularly useful in their own lives. Because these texts were geared for a specific audience, we have noted the parish, the Gospel text, the occasion when they were delivered . . . as much as we were able.

The spoken word doesn't always translate easily or well into the written sentence, so some portions have been edited. But great care has been taken to stay true to the words and spirit of his message.

This book is the result of the work of three persons who constitute the committee which has kept Ken's *Little Books* series alive after his death in 2004: Sr. Nancy Ayotte, IHM, Catherine Haven, and Leona Jones.

But they did not work alone. In the more than 10 years since Ken's death, they have received the encouragement, support, prayers, and advice of many folks both within and without the Diocese of Saginaw. We are grateful to Fr. Bob Byrne, Fr. Bill Taylor, and Nancy Driscoll. We are also grateful to Bishop Tom Gumbleton of the Archdiocese of Detroit, to whom Ken bequeathed his papers, and who has been generous and supportive of our work.

Part I:
I am the seventh of nine children . . .

I am the seventh of nine children ...

—⚍—

As the infant was about to be baptized, the priest turned to the child's father and asked, "What is the baby's name?"

The man replied, "Kenneth."

The priest said, "Kenneth is not a saint's name."

Andrew Untener replied, "Then he'll be the first one."

Kenneth Edward Untener was born on August 3, 1937, in Detroit, Michigan.

Of Hungarian descent, he was the seventh child of Andrew and Anna Krayniak Untener. His dad was a World War I veteran, one of the Polar Bear Brigade that had fought in Russia. Andrew Untener died in 1975 (while Ken was in Rome defending his doctoral thesis), five years before his son became bishop. Anna Untener was a home-maker who kept busy raising nine children.

Ken and his brothers and sisters attended St. Charles Borromeo Grade and High School on Detroit's east side. The schools were staffed by the Sisters Servants of the Immaculate Heart of Mary, a religious order his eldest sister, Mary Ann, entered in 1945.

Ken did well in school. He was elected class president his senior year, yet always joked about his disappointment at never being the window pole boy in first grade. He was too short and the windows were too tall for him to open and close – even with the window pole. Years later at the 25th anniversary of his ordination, his first grade teacher, Sr. Anna Mae Nadeau, presented him with his very own window pole embellished with a festive bow.

As one of the younger children in the Untener family, Ken received the hand-me-downs from his older brothers. A typical middle child, he was often a peacemaker . . . when he wasn't the instigator.

"I do not enjoy conflict," he once told a reporter. "I would not make a very good labor negotiator. When it's thrust upon me, I deal with it the best that I can."

Over the years, in homilies as well as in conversations with friends, Ken often thanked his family for the gift of his faith: "You know who has nurtured my faith more than anyone else? My mother and my dad . . . and some other people along the way who were regular folks, but who were just trying to do their best to love God and love their neighbor. People who tried to spin out in their own lives the story of the life of Jesus . . . who were members of this imperfect Church and who knew and loved its customs and traditions.

"There is no question that they have touched my heart and shaped my faith more than anything."

Accepting God's gifts

---

*A*s I thought about Mark 10:2-16 (in which Jesus is questioned about marriage and divorce) and the feast of St. Francis of Assisi, a story came back to me that I have never told before and one which I had forgotten. It happened when I was perhaps six, seven or eight years old.

Now you must understand that my family was not poor. There were nine children, and my dad worked for the City of Detroit. We didn't have much money, but we had the basic necessities of life. We didn't always dress very well, and most of the clothes we had were hand-me-downs.

Well, one night we were surprised by a knock at the door and a couple of people came in with armfuls of clothes. They were from the parish and, with great smiles on their faces, were bringing these clothes for the Untener children. It was a total surprise. They didn't stay long. They just set this pile of clothes on the dining room table, said a few nice things, and then left.

We kids thought it was terrific. We started tearing into the pile of clothes and finding things that we liked, looking for a new jacket and all those kinds of things that kids do. Then I remember seeing my mother just sort of slumped into a chair, sitting there crying. She didn't cry very often, and that's one of the reasons why I remember it so well.

Why was she crying? Well, she must have been touched by the goodness of whoever it was who brought the clothes. But I knew that wasn't the biggest reason why she was crying.

She was crying because she didn't want to be on the receiving end of charity. We weren't poor – we really weren't *that* poor – and no one really wants to be on the receiving end of gifts like that. (Once you've been there for a while, you might get used to it, but the first time is very, very hard.)

It is hard to be a person who simply receives gifts that they cannot repay. It's hard to need gifts. Even when it comes to God, we'd like to pretend that we deserve what God gives us and that we have partially earned it. God was dealing with precisely that problem when he said we have to learn to accept the kingdom of God as a little child.

St. Francis of Assisi learned how to do it. He had been the son of a rich family, but then he gave it all up and unabashedly became poor. In Italy they call him *Il Poverello* – the Little Poor One. He received the handouts that people gave him and his community, and he received the handouts from God.

All of this affected him, and he treated the rest of creation that way. He gave the gift of his love and compassion and kindness to all of God's little ones – the birds of the sky and the rich people and everyone.

It is easy to say that we must learn to accept God's gifts for what they are.

The truth of the matter is: It's hard to accept a gift when we cannot repay with another gift, and when we don't deserve it, and when we are not an equal.

Twenty-seventh Sunday in Ordinary Time/B cycle; Mk 10:2-16; St. Francis Home for older persons in Saginaw; October 2, 1988.

First Communion

When I made my first Communion (and as I learned about Communion), all the emphasis was really on what happened *before* I received Communion – that this bread and wine truly became the body and blood of Jesus, that I was to prepare myself to receive it worthily, and that I was to receive it without touching it with my teeth.

Wouldn't it be interesting if most or all of the emphasis had been on what happened *after* I received Communion?

What if my second-grade teachers had said to me: "Now when you receive this, something is going to happen to you. Once you receive the body of the Lord, there will be no more Anglo and no more Hispanic. There will be no more rich, no more poor, no more black, white, bad, good. It shall all be the Body of Christ. When you receive this, something happens."

Imagine the effect that would have had on me.

Holy Thursday at the Cathedral of Mary of the Assumption in Saginaw; March 23, 1989.

High shoes in third grade

When I was in about the third grade, it was time for a new pair of shoes so my mother took me downtown to buy some.

Up until then I had to wear "high shoes" and I desperately wanted "low shoes."

I figured that this would be the breakthrough.

Wouldn't you know, my mother went and bought me high shoes. I didn't even want to go to school the next day. I wasn't worried about the bare necessity of *having* shoes on my feet. I was worried about the *kind* of shoes.

Those are the kinds of things we worry about – the things that make us acceptable and important to others.

We don't worry simply about having clothes on our back; we worry about the kind of clothes. We don't worry simply about having a roof over our head; we worry about the kind of house. We don't worry simply about transportation; we worry about the kind of car.

There are a hundred ways in which we measure the importance of ourselves and others – the kind of job, car, house, clothes.

Come the kingdom, these will be as unimportant as high shoes in third grade.

Eighth Sunday in Ordinary Time/A cycle; Mt 6:24-34; pre-Lenten televised Mass 1987.

Mother's Day gift

I remember one Mother's Day back when I was in the second or third grade.

I'm the seventh of nine children, and the next one above me is my brother, about two years older.

A couple of weeks before Mother's Day, he came up with this idea.

He said, "Let's buy mother a box of Sanders chocolate candy."

She loved that candy. Of course, so did we.

Trouble is, we didn't have any money, but he had a plan.

We used to get a dime every school day so that we could buy milk to drink with our bologna sandwich at lunch.

My brother said, "Now here's what we're going to do. The box of candy costs just a little more than two dollars. We're going to skip the milk at lunch for the next couple of weeks. We'll save those dimes, and then we'll have enough money for a box of candy."

So we did.

We'd get home from school and stash the dimes in a special hiding place. About every three hours, we'd count it to see how much we had.

The days went by and on the Friday before Mother's Day, as our dad was driving us home from school, we told him to stop at Sanders Confectionary Store because we were going to buy mother a box of chocolate candy.

He was surprised and asked where we got the money (he wanted to be sure we weren't out stealing cars). We told him the whole story. Then we went inside the Sanders store, plunked down the 24 dimes, and came out with the candy.

Come the big day, we gave our mother the big gift. She was delighted . . . and surprised.

Looking back, I figure that after we had given her the candy, our dad told her how we had saved up the money because later that same day our mother came to us. She thanked us again, and there were tears running down her cheeks.

My brother and I (with our great insight into human nature) said to ourselves, "What's she crying about? She got a box of candy."

There came a time, of course, when we were old enough to understand.

The truth is, as much as we wanted that chocolate milk at lunch, we wanted even more to give this gift to our mother. The good feeling and the excitement of doing that were even more important than having chocolate milk at lunch.

Life can be very busy these days, and it's not always filled with things we like to do. Our big task on a given day may be wearisome – an annoyance, a bother, a chore, an inconvenience, an aggravation, a hassle. We may not like our job. Or we may be struggling with a difficult marriage, or health problems, or – lots of things. There's many a day when a lot of what we do – *most* of what we do – seems just a chore.

While thinking about Mother's Day, a great solution for all this dawned on me. We simply need to think of children working hard to do something for their mothers on Mother's Day. Then we simply remember that what we do all day, we're doing for God.

God put us here for a purpose. We may not always know what it is, but if we do our best with what lies before us each day, we are fulfilling God's purpose.

Which means we're doing it for God.

If I stop and think of that just briefly at the beginning of the day, and a couple of times during the day . . . why, it would make a great difference. I tried it the last couple of days, and, do you know what? It works.

Fourth Sunday of Easter/B cycle; Jn 10:11-18.

Class reunion

A while back I received an invitation to a great high school reunion at St. Charles Borromeo on the east side of Detroit. The class of 1940 was going to host it because their class was celebrating its 50th year.

My class graduated in 1955. Our school was closed a long time ago, so the class of 1940 wanted everyone to come and celebrate a grand reunion.

I got to thinking. Do you think that back in 1955, I could have looked at my class and distinguished the weeds from the wheat?

Imagine back to your high school graduating class (or any class you were part of), and think of how people looked to you then, and (if you've ever had a get-together since then) how differently you see the people now.

We've had a couple of reunions, and I have been so surprised to see how differently I looked at classmates now. Back in high school, the people that you thought had everything that you thought people who are popular ought to have – fellows who were great on the football team back then were heroes and popular – now a lot of them have great big pot bellies.

And the girls that I thought were so much fun to be with, and the ones that I thought were, you know, not the most popular – oftentimes that's reversed and their personalities have emerged. You see them so differently.

Even the teachers. There were the teachers that we thought were nice, and then there were the others we thought were trained in a Nazi boot camp. You look back and are now grateful to some of them for the discipline and the good, solid formation that they gave.

You see it all so differently.

Jesus tells us that when we have the great reunion in the kingdom of God, people will look a lot different. Just as I have a different perspective 35 years after graduating from high school, the perspective in the kingdom will be so much wider. We will understand things that we never understood before. We will see everything differently.

I have to be careful because there is this tendency to judge people, and you can't. There are things that are right and wrong, and we know what those are and we should hold them. But we shouldn't judge the hearts of the people around us.

In my 27 years of priesthood, I have been brought into the lives of a wider range of people than most other people would. I have worked with and come to know people who have done awful things. But when I talked to them and I heard their stories, I saw flashes of goodness there. What they did was terribly wrong, but I wonder if deep down when they come before the Lord, they're not going to be holier than I am.

You just can't know the whole story and the heart of people.

Come the great class reunion in the kingdom, we'll all look a lot different. For now, we must accept one another, always, as brothers and sisters in the same family . . . as equal.

And never, never claim to know the weeds from the wheat.

Sixteenth Sunday in Ordinary Time/A cycle; Mt 13:24-30; St. Andrew Parish, Holy Rosary Parish, and Our Lady Help of Christian Parish in Saginaw; July 22, 1990.

Neighborhood pool halls

*P*ool halls have a distinctive ambience. You can always expect an interesting mixture of people.

At the pool hall I went to many years ago in downtown Detroit, they had some billiard tables, and that was a touch of class. Some fellows even wore suits. But there was still a place for the rest of us.

There was quite a collection of people – young and old, dressed up and dirty, accomplished cue artists and sloppers, and some who just hung around. No one felt out of place. Everyone figured the others had a right to be there. It was what you might call the "anticipated ambience" of a pool hall.

It was somewhat the same at a Tiger ballgame when you sat in the bleachers. That's where we always sat when my dad took us. He told us the bleachers gave you the best view of all the action on the field. Besides, that's where the real fans were (he didn't mention the tickets were also cheaper). Bleacher folks were quite a cross-section of humanity. My dad prepared us for this with his talk about the "real fans" being there, and we didn't mind a bit.

What is the anticipated ambience of our parish church? The people tend to be clean-cut, well-behaved, decent-living, middle-class, socially acceptable. They're my family and friends . . . my kind of people.

There are some other types too, but not many are in most parishes. Many less socially and/or less religiously acceptable people don't figure a church is the kind of place they ought to be. Parishes don't intentionally screen these people out. It just works out that way.

Whatever the cause, there's a big difference between the anticipated ambience of the pool hall or the bleachers, and the average parish church.

What is the anticipated ambience around Jesus?

Shepherds are there at his birth, and they were definitely the bleacher crowd. In his public ministry, Jesus allows lepers near him, and even touches them. Troublesome demoniacs are occasionally there carrying on in a way you wouldn't want at a refined gathering. A paralytic comes through the roof. Blind men shout to get his attention. A sinful woman interrupts a meal with tears and oil. Hungry crowds are irksome to the disciples, and so is the tenacious Canaanite woman.

Jesus cautions about being too quick to sort the fish or pull up the weeds: "Large crowds of people came to him bringing with them cripples, the deformed, the blind, the mute and many others." Jesus tells the story about the beggar covered with sores who could not eat at the rich man's table. He shocks his disciples by conversing publicly with a woman (a Samaritan, no less). He says that when you give a dinner, you should invite beggars.

The truth is, I'm not altogether comfortable with people like that *at church*. I would be at a pool hall, or in the bleachers, but not at church. I'm not conditioned for it. My dad had to prepare us for church the same way he did for the bleachers.

Jesus includes in his company a lot of people who aren't used to being included in the synagogues or dinner gatherings of his time. Should our parishes be more that way? Should they include what some people would call "riff-raff?"

I was thinking about this on a DC-10 headed for the West Coast. I took a good look around the plane and concluded that these were the kind of people who would make up a typical Sunday congregation. Then I pictured the people around Jesus, looked around the plane again, and said to myself: "No, not enough riff-raff."

We need to find ways to make our parishes more inclusive of social and ecclesial misfits. They have to feel that this is their home as much as ours.

Perhaps it's the only significant place in the world where they can feel that way.

Perhaps it is the only way I can experience firsthand the implications of Jesus' teaching about "who is my neighbor."

Advent 1984.

Uncle Julius

I'd like to tell you the story of my Uncle Julius, God rest him. Uncle Julius (I suppose there is a person like this in every family) was a drifter. Uncle Julius never held a job, and Uncle Julius drank a little too much.

But every now and then, he'd show up and (I remember as a little kid) we all loved him. He was kindly and a very good person. He was compassionate and understanding.

He just could never get his life together.

We always loved it when he showed up – of course, you never knew *when* he was going to show up. He'd drift in from out of town on a Greyhound bus. He's the one who taught me how to play the horses . . . but only when I was of age.

My mother was worried about Uncle Julius because he didn't take very good care of himself. Every now and then you'd hear from him . . . but you'd never know when. Sometimes he'd call up on holidays from some state.

One time she was talking to him on the telephone and he said he'd been sick for some time. She was very concerned.

She said, "Have you seen a doctor?"

He said, "Well, no."

She said, "Why not?"

He said, "You see, I've got to figure out what's wrong with me so I know which doctor to go to."

She tried to explain to him that that's why you go to a doctor, to find out what's wrong with you and let them work it out.

It seems to me that we have that attitude sometimes toward being part of the Church, part of the Eucharist: You're supposed to get your act together and *then* come.

I always like to use the analogy of Weight Watchers for the Church. People go to Weight Watchers because they need help. It would be interesting for someone (like a Pharisee) to stand outside the Weight

Watchers meeting and say, "Look at all those hypocrites going in there to Weight Watchers and they're all overweight."

You'd say, "That's why they go."

Look at all the hypocrites coming to church and not one of them is perfect.

That's why we go.

Twenty-sixth Sunday in Ordinary Time/A cycle; Mt 21:28-32; SS. Peter and Paul Parish, Saginaw; September 26/27, 1987.

Polar Bear brigade

My dad fought in the First World War in a contingent of Detroit soldiers that was sent to Russia. They were known as the "Polar Bears."

After my dad died in 1975 at the age of 80, we found among his things a journal that he had kept while he was in the army. It was fascinating to read a handwritten journal – every day an entry – as he sailed across the ocean, worked his way over to Russia, and then marched into the heart of Russia and engaged in battle.

In the course of reading this journal (it lasted several years), you would get to know several of his friends in the army, and then you would read how some of his friends got killed.

I thought to myself, my dad could have been killed way back then, and I would not be here.

On Memorial Day weekend, you think about things like that and people who were killed. We are all touched by war. We've had friends, relatives, people we know, killed in wars.

I wonder what would happen if any of them could come back and talk to us? What advice would they have? Would they see things differently – about life, about the world, about politics, about what is important, about peace? I'm sure that they would have something to say, with a different perspective on it all, and we would be all ears to listen.

One of the reasons I thought of all that is because of the Gospel when Jesus says to his disciples, "I'm going to come back. I have more to say to you. There's more to say and you can't yet understand it. So I will come back to you and I will send my Spirit, and the Spirit will teach you."

Jesus said that: "He will teach you, and remind you of all that I have taught you."

That's a fascinating thing to remember. That's part of our belief.

Sixth Sunday of Easter/C cycle; Jn 14:23-29; confirmation at Sacred Heart Parish in Caro, St. Joseph Parish in Rapson, St. Frances Cabrini Parish in Vassar, and St. Bernard Parish in Millington; May 24/25, 1992.

My dad's death

---

1 remember when my dad died back in 1975. He died suddenly and he was the first family member to die (since then I have experienced the death of one of my sisters).

A couple of days after the funeral, we went to the cemetery to see how the grave had been taken care of. We were just standing there, sort of in silence for a while, and I was next to my younger sister.

I figured it was probably a gripping thing, this first visit to the grave, and so I asked her how she was doing.

She said, "Just fine. I don't believe he's here anyway. He's with God."

Now my sister isn't given to making a lot of pious statements. She was simply speaking her belief about what happens after death. She said it pretty well, and it expressed my belief, too.

The Church never has quite figured out the delay between dying and going to the Lord as a "soul" and then later on experiencing the fullness of risen life.

The belief in Mary's assumption, newly defined just a few years ago, may be the leading edge of a clearer understanding. It may express what happens to everyone at death – they go to the Lord and they go there as a complete human being, spirit, flesh, and blood in its risen state.

To tell the truth, that's what I believe about my dad.

Vigil of the Assumption; Lk 11:27-28.

My sister Alice

————————

When I told some members of my family that I wanted to use the Gospel of the laborers in the vineyard for my sister's funeral, they thought maybe I needed a saliva test.

It wasn't their favorite Gospel, and they didn't think it had much to do with a funeral. I told them that it was a bit different but that I could explain its application. They said okay, as long as I didn't take forever trying to explain it.

In order to understand how the Gospel fits, you have to understand something about my sister Alice.

In a sense, a card symbolized her whole life. The card testified that she donated her body to science. Alice was very proud of that. You see, Alice was an independent thinker and an independent kind of person. To donate your body to medicine is a very independent thing to do. She told us about it, and we knew that when she died, we were to call this phone number and they would take the body.

But when she died, they didn't want her body. Her body was in such poor condition from years of sickness that they couldn't use it.

That final irony symbolizes a great deal about Alice's life.

When she was young, Alice was a lively person, who laughed and sang a lot, and was an asset to any party. She dropped out of college because, as she said, it wasn't her thing. She loved to cook and she loved housekeeping, and she wanted to get married and have children. So, she went out and got a job.

One day, when she was 19, she was the victim of a violent crime. Within a year, she was only a shadow of herself. She struggled through that inch by inch and it took a long time – maybe 10 years. It was a while before she could hold a job, or drive a car, or be independent. But she got one job after another, and then went to school at night learning stenotyping so she could be a court reporter.

At long last she made it. She had a profession and she could be independent, and she was very proud of that.

Then, all of a sudden, from out of the blue she discovered she had lupus. None of us had ever heard of that disease. It's a tough one. It attacks one thing after another in your system, and it is a constant battle to try to keep it under control.

Alice fought lupus for 12 years. It was an up-and-down struggle, and it took its toll. It ruined her hands and cost her the speed she needed to be a court reporter.

She tried to be a legal secretary, figuring she could draw upon her experience with legal terms and legal procedures. But then it was her eyes. Lupus gradually ruined them so that she couldn't even see to type. By the time she died, she could barely see at all.

There is more to her story (and more than I know), but that gives you enough to know the pattern of Alice's life. Try as she may, everything turned out wrong.

Even her attempted gift of her body to science.

And now this Gospel. To understand this Gospel, you have to realize that the laborers who did not get hired until late in the afternoon were anything but lazy, shiftless people. They had been in that village square since early dawn hoping to be hired. And when, late in the afternoon, the master asked them why they were still there, they answered, "Nobody would hire us." They wanted work and needed work, but were passed over.

Now I guess it makes a great deal of difference in whose shoes you place yourself when you read this Gospel. Usually we think about the poor fellows who worked all day.

But what if I put myself in the shoes of the ones who didn't? They stood there all day long and didn't have the good luck to be hired. They stood there and went through the embarrassment of being passed over . . . of wanting to work but not being able to work.

Which is harder: To want to work and need work, yet not be able to work? Or to work all day? Which is harder: To want to be independent and have your own place and take care of it and not be able to? Or to go through all the work and expense of maintaining an apartment or a flat or a home?

That litany could go on and on.

As I said, there is more to Alice's story than I know. Each of us has our own litany, because each of us has faced setbacks and failures in our own lives. When we think about those setbacks in our life – the hard luck – whose shoes would we place ourselves in as we read this Gospel? Whose shoes would we put Alice in?

Alice watched a lot of life pass her by. She stood in that village square and was passed over many times. She missed a lot of paydays, and I don't mean just the kind of paydays when you get a check (she missed a lot of those, too). I mean the personal paydays – the personal payoff you get from accomplishing things you want to do, from being needed by others, from being significant in people's lives.

Alice missed a lot of those paydays, and it wasn't fair.

In the Gospel, the master was fair. We would have paid off simply by looking at externals. The master could read hearts, and he used that ability to be fairer than ever we could be.

We shouldn't take our "luck" too seriously. I use the word "luck" deliberately. There is a lot of that in our life – good luck and bad luck. God doesn't necessarily send every specific turn of events into our lives. God leaves us free in a free world, and simply promises to be with us no matter what happens.

Sometimes we take our good luck too seriously. We begin to think that it is all our own accomplishment. That was the mistake of the laborers in the Gospel who were hired early. They actually thought that they were better than the others.

They weren't. They were just lucky.

We should be grateful for any good fortune we have, but we should never take it too seriously. And we shouldn't take the bad luck too seriously either.

That was one thing about Alice. She never let all those setbacks overwhelm her. She never let them turn her bitter. Sometimes she even laughed about them. She never took her bad luck too seriously . . . and we can learn something from that.

Funeral Mass for Alice Untener; August 1978; Mt. 20:1-15.

Piano player

I learned to play piano when I was in grade school. I learned the classics and I learned the scales and I learned the chords, and I learned how to read music.

I also learned how to take all that I had learned and be able to play my own music. I can fool around and play things that come to my mind. I can play Elvis Presley classically. That's what I learned to do when I play piano, and if I was any good at it, I would set a big glass goblet on the piano and put a dollar bill in it.

When I learned to play piano, my teachers didn't teach me how to play one song. They taught me how to play the piano. Now I play songs they never knew because new songs are always being written. When I hear Billy Joel or someone on the radio, I can sit down and I play that. It takes me a while to figure it out but I can do it.

Imagine if my teachers had just taught me one song. You could teach anybody one song, and they could play that one song for the rest of their lives and never know how to play the piano.

But my teachers taught me how to play the piano. You could tell I had good teachers. They loved music and they gave me a love for music.

But that's not all.

I had older brothers and sisters. I had my brother, Bob, who could sing like a lark. I grew up hearing the sound of music in the air. I had an older sister, Rita, who played the piano. I remember growing up and listening to her play the piano and I remember the family gathering around the piano and singing songs.

I remember my parents – neither of them could play the piano but they loved music – and I could see their faces light up when we sang. When I learned to play the piano, I could see their faces light up. They went to the recitals and they paid the money and they bought a piano. There was music in the air at home.

I sometimes worry whether or not the music of God – faith – is in the air enough at home. I sometimes worry how often prayers are said, and where they are said – at the table or at the bedside.

I am sometimes sorry about the loss of religious customs, of blessings. I sometimes worry how many religious images there are – good ones like the cross and the images of the Last Supper – in homes.

I learned to play the piano because I had good teachers, but also because it was in the air at home. Because of that, I learned to love music. Now I can play new music and I can always learn and make new arrangements.

My prayer for youngsters is that they will have good teachers (as I had good teachers in music), that they will see the same faith shine on the faces of people at home, and that the sound of God's music will be in the air.

Nobody can take youngsters and put them, for sure, on the right course. But what we can do is steep them in the traditions, steep them in an understanding of the music of faith, and give them a love for that music. We can teach them not just one song, but all the music of God.

School Family Mass at St. Stephen Parish in Saginaw; Mk 16:15-18; January 24, 1995.

Story of fear

M y brother told me a story about his in-laws who are elderly and live alone.

It was during the bitter cold of January and they had their furnace cleaned.

The people who cleaned it said, "You know, you've got a problem here. There's a carbon monoxide leak. You can't smell it, and it's only a little leak. It probably wouldn't affect you, but it could kill your dog."

There was more.

"There are also a couple of problems with the furnace. It could go out, and in the thick of winter, that could be very bad."

You can guess their reaction: Fear.

So they had these people fix the furnace. It cost $2,500. They could have bought a new furnace for less. My brother found out about it, brought in an expert who looked it over and said, "There was nothing wrong with the furnace."

This sort of thing goes on all the time. People get taken because of fear. It happens with car repairs, door-to-door sales, or through the mail. People, often older people, get taken. We could all tell stories.

The problem is fear.

People prey upon fear in the Church today.

I can't tell you how many times in recent years people have said to me, "I've heard the United States bishops are trying to break off from Rome and form an American Church." I don't know of and have never heard of one single bishop who would even entertain the remote possibility of doing such a thing. There's no more truth to that than the supposed repairs needed by that elderly couple's furnace. But it preys upon the same thing: Fear.

I've read in some publications that there are cardinals who have infiltrated the Vatican and who are communist or belong to the Mafia or some other subversive group. People, especially elderly people upon whom these publications prey, become frightened. Nothing could be further from the truth; there is no basis . . . any more than the furnace that needed $2,500 to be fixed. But fear does that to people, and there are those who prey upon people's fear.

Then there are reports of visions that tell of awful things in the Church, or of terrible calamities to come upon our world – days of darkness, wars, plagues, disease, earthquakes. I get them in the mail all the time, terrifying messages from heaven. They prey upon people's fear.

These publications claim to have heaven-sent warnings from Jesus or Mary or other saints. Some warn that even the pope is being taken in and is going in the wrong direction because he dares to gather people of all faiths to pray for peace. Others claim to be vigilantes defending the pope against underground movements of bishops and priests, or for that matter, above ground waves of rebellious bishops and priests who are working for Satan.

These are the religious versions of the checkout line tabloids. They are bizarre, totally false, sometimes hate-filled. They have this in common: They lack Church approval, even though they may set themselves up as defenders of the Church. They also have something else in common: They prey upon people's fear. They don't deal with facts, issues. They deal with rumors, hearsay, and fear.

It's a terrible thing to prey on people's fear, and it's a terrible thing for us to give into fear, as though Jesus is far away and helpless.

Jesus isn't a spectator watching from a distance. Jesus is in the boat, just as he was with the apostles when the storm hit. Instead of worrying that we are sinking, we need to let the words of Jesus sink in: "Take courage. Do not be afraid. It is I . . . know that I am with you all days, even to the end of the age."

Nineteenth Sunday in Ordinary Time/A cycle; Mt 14:22-33; Cathedral of Mary of the Assumption in Saginaw; seminarian commitment; August 10, 1996.

God sings over me

In Zephaniah 3:14-18, there is a line that in my 34 years as a priest, I never noticed.

It's a beautiful image. It says: "The Lord your God is in your midst. The Lord your God will rejoice over you with singing."

God sings over me. When I think about that, probably the last time somebody sang over me (or at least the image that comes most clearly to mind) is when I was a little child. You know how parents hold their children and sing to them? That came home to me so strikingly years ago.

I'm the seventh of nine children. The next brother up from me is my brother, Dick. We're the closest in age.

Most of the people in my family played a musical instrument or something . . . except my brother, Dick. He was proud to be able to play the radio. I think the only song he knew was "Happy Birthday."

Well, he had his first daughter. She was four or five months old, and we were visiting. It was late at night. He held his daughter and I saw him across the room. He was singing to her. It was a beautiful thing. It was the most astounding thing I ever saw.

When I think of myself being held by God that way, and God singing over me, I realize how precious I am to God, how much God loves me, and how much God takes care of me.

Second Sunday of Advent/C cycle; Lk 3:101-18; St. Casimir/St. George Parish in Saginaw; December 13-14, 1997.

Blowing out the candle

I went down to Detroit and celebrated the wedding of one of my nieces.

It was a very nice ceremony. They had been planning it for a long time and wanted everything to be right.

One of the things that was part of the ceremony was a custom that is picking up momentum: The candle ceremony.

Just after the couple exchanges vows and becomes, in fact, husband and wife, they go up to the altar where there are two lit candles and an unlit candle in the middle. They take a taper and light it from each of the lit candles (each of those candles representing their own individual lives). Together, they light the middle candle, which symbolizes those two lives becoming one. Then they blow out the two candles to show that those individual lives are no more, but in that sense have become one life.

At the reception, a woman whom I didn't know came up to me and said, "You know what the best part of that whole ceremony was? When they blew out those candles." (She didn't say it was the sermon or the music – and there were trumpets – and there was everything you could think of, with the setting and all.)

She said, "I've been married for a long time and it's very true. You have to blow out the candle of your own life, and it's difficult. The truest part of that whole ceremony was when they had to blow out the individual candles."

I think that captures what Jesus was saying when he said that a grain of wheat has to fall to the ground and die. Or when he said that people who love their lives lose them, while people who hate their lives in this world preserve them for life eternal.

I wouldn't want anyone to think that a good Christian is someone who doesn't love life. But there is a difference between clutching life to oneself and learning to blow out the candle of our own grasping selfishness so that we can go out and enjoy life.

That's the way Jesus lived . . . the way Jesus died. That's the way Jesus is telling us, "I want you to be happy. You were never made to be just one candle, preserving the flame all to yourself, as though you were the center of the universe, the only person. I made you to be part of a grand family called the human race."

There's a sinful instinct in all us to make ourselves the center of the universe. In other words, to care for Number One, me, and to only care about myself.

Jesus is saying that we've got to blow out the candle a lot. If we're ever going to discover the beauty of other people, we've got to shut up and listen. We've got to blow out our own candle. If we are ever going to discover what kind of person we were made to be, we've got to blow out the candle of our own possessiveness and enjoy the thrill of giving things away.

Anyone who has lived in a family of more than one person knows that if you want to enjoy family life, you've got to blow out the candle a lot to be part of it.

Fifth Sunday of Lent/B cycle; Jn 12:20-33.

A successful family

I come from a large family.

My father's brother also had a large family, and every couple of years both families get together for a "cousins convention."

There are about 70 or 80 of us, four generations. We rent cabins and spend a week together. It's quite an extended family.

We have a good family. However, in our adult family there are all the problems you find in any family. There is divorce, sickness, alcohol abuse, bad feelings and rifts, crime, economic problems, suicide . . . to mention a few. These are the things that are part of the life of any extended family.

Sometimes we forget that. Other families look so good – tidy house, trimmed front lawn, smiles on their faces – and we think all is well. Indeed, all may be well, but you can be sure that these kinds of problems are in their extended family. They are part of every good family.

You become a good family by learning how to deal with these things.

Now, there is nothing worse than a family fight, because family fights can start over something very small, get serious very quickly, and last a lifetime. I'm not sure why that is, but I know it's so.

One of my cousins didn't even attend his father's funeral and neither we nor his own family ever knew why. We knew there was a fight, but we didn't know what caused it. Some thought it had to do with something his father said way back when he got married. What a terrible shame. But that's what happens in family fights.

A successful family is one that somehow manages to make do and hold together, despite differences and wounds. Never, never let a rift become a wall. It takes some creativity and a lot of patience, but it can be done . . . and we will often have to take the initiative.

We don't have to condone everything that a person does, but, on the other hand, we don't have to condemn the person either.

The words and actions of Jesus when they brought the woman caught in adultery to him could be particularly appropriate for dealing with family members who do things we cannot condone. When the crowd ready to stone her had drifted away, Jesus said to her, "Has no one condemned you?" She replied, "No one, sir." Then Jesus said, "Nor do I condemn you."

Everyone is part of an extended family, and everyone has a responsibility to contribute to married life. Not simply parents. Not simply married people. Our society is built on families. Our country is built on families. They are critical to the health of the human race. Recently I was discussing crime with an FBI agent. He said that one good family can do more to prevent crime than he could do in a lifetime.

The Lord, who dealt with his own kinship group, understands from firsthand experience all the problems involved.

Feast of the Holy Family/A cycle; Mt 2:13-15, 19-23; Holy Family Parish in Saginaw; December 27, 1992.

Family obligation

*D*uring the past 25 years, many Catholics have drifted away from the Eucharist.

I know some of them very well. Some are part of my extended family and acquaintances. Some come hardly at all. Some come only now and then.

A short while back, I was talking to someone who had drifted away from regular participation in the Eucharist. He said something like this:

"Well, I had trouble with some of the things going on in the Church. I didn't like the way they did liturgy at our parish. I really got nothing out of it. But it's not as though I've turned my back on God or on Jesus. I still feel very close to them. You can be close to God and to Jesus anywhere. Sometimes I pray when I'm driving."

My response to him went something like this:

"I think you are a good person, and I think you really have not turned your back on God. But I don't think you can call yourself a 'disciple of the Lord' any more than the disciples who drifted away from Jesus could still call themselves disciples.

"You may 'like' Jesus, but you've drifted away from following him. Jesus sat at the table with his disciples and said to them and to his disciples of all ages: 'Do this in memory of me.' The 'do' involved coming to the eucharistic table. You've chosen not to do that. Jesus said to his disciples around the table and to the disciples of every age: 'Take and eat . . . take and drink.' You've chosen not to do that. This is part of following him, of being a disciple. You've drifted away from being a disciple of Jesus."

It was very interesting. This had never occurred to him (actually, it had never occurred to me to put it this way before). He hadn't for a moment thought that he had moved away from following Jesus. He thought he had simply backed away from the Church, which was an unnecessary institution that got between him and Jesus.

He said, "I have to think about all that."

It has been my experience that people can get very angry at the Church and upset with leaders in the Church and so on. But people really do love Jesus. People really do believe in what he taught and how he lived. People want to be close to him. Somehow they think about this in sort of a vague way and forget that Jesus has expectations of his disciples. One of the clear expectations is "Do this in memory of me." I think this needs to be made clearer.

I come from a large family and many of them still live in the Detroit area. Before my mother died a couple of years ago, the family always got together on Christmas afternoon.

Now, after I have celebrated a midnight Mass, gotten in very late, then celebrated some Masses in the morning, then gone to St. Mary's Hospital to visit the people there (I do that every Christmas because I figure if you're in a hospital on Christmas Day you deserve a visitor) – when all that was finished, the last thing I wanted to do was to get into my car and drive for two hours down to the Detroit area. What I really wanted to do was go to wherever I was living and have a beer and watch a football game.

But I didn't do that.

Why? Because my family expected me to be there.

They could have had a good time without me and there would be plenty of them there. But they expected me. We all expected each other. It was that expectation, that "obligation" that nudged me to get into the car and drive for two hours. Of course, after doing it, I was always glad I did. But sometimes I need that nudge.

An "obligation" isn't all that bad.

Twenty-first Sunday in Ordinary Time/B cycle; Jn 6:60-69; Assumption of the Blessed Virgin Mary Parish in Bridgeport.

New way of doing Christmas

When I was growing up, Christmas was wonderful.

The whole family was always together. We had our own customs and our own way of doing Christmas. We opened our presents . . . but not before Christmas morning. I know some families could open gifts Christmas Eve (I always thought those were the lucky kids) but we opened ours on Christmas morning. We had our own way of trimming the tree on Christmas Eve.

I just have the happiest memories of that. When my older brothers were away at college or in the service, they would come home for Christmas.

Then our family grew. My brothers and sisters started getting married, and some problems developed: Whose house do you go to on Christmas: Your wife's or your husband's? And when are we going to have our own Christmas?

My mother and dad wanted everybody over, naturally – you know the story – so the Unteners found a new way of doing Christmas. We stopped trying to say, "Well, this is the way we have always done it," and let them have their own Christmas.

And they do.

The entire family doesn't get together at Christmas, because each family has its own customs that they've developed. It's the same Christmas, but a new way of doing it. Our family was able to leave behind being together, and I'm sure it was hard for my mother and dad to leave that behind.

But we found a new way of getting together. We get together twice a summer for a big family ballgame, with a cookout afterwards. All the kids and everybody have a great time. That's the way we've found to continue getting together, by changing and finding a new way of doing it – because things are different now. (I'm also the commissioner of the Untener Baseball League. I make all the rules, and my team always wins!)

It's hard to move on. It's hard to take the risks of adventure – to do it personally and to do it as a Church. The Church has always struggled to live up to Jesus' marching orders. It's hard.

It's always hard to travel light.

It's always hard to leave things behind.

It's always hard to take the risks and the adventures and the surprise of turning a corner and trying to follow the Lord where he's taking you – down roads you may not know very well.

Fifteenth Sunday in Ordinary Time/B cycle; Mk 6:7-13.

Times when I felt important

I recently asked myself, When in my life did I feel important?
Now you might say: Well, it must have been one of those big deals
that you did as a bishop. You know, you come here to Saginaw and
you're installed as the bishop of the diocese at the Civic Center with
6,000 people there . . .

I stand as the bishop. I stand as a symbol for many things . . . and
I'm happy to do that. But that's not the kind of importance I'm talking
about. I'm talking about where you feel that you have importance and
are special to people and to God.

I began to think, "What *were* the times in my life when I felt important?"

Ten years ago, my dad died. I'll never forget when at the funeral
I saw some people that I didn't think had to come. They came from
a long ways. They were friends of mine, and they had taken a day
off work and come there just for me – that was some kind of feeling.
That's what I mean by feeling important.

I remember, as a little child, I felt important on my birthday. I was
the seventh of nine kids, and for a lot of us on our birthday we had
kind of a ritual.

At supper, when it was time for dessert, my mother always sent
the person whose birthday it was off to do an errand. We all knew it
was phony but it was a ritual. You went off to do the errand – go to
the basement and get such-and-such – and while you were gone, they
brought the cake out and the presents. Your brothers and sisters whom
you were with all year long all smiled and sang to you and there was
that feeling of importance.

I can remember another time – the first time my parents ever came
to see me play hockey (by then, I was in high school). Back then, kids'
sports were a lot different than they are now. Parents didn't come and
argue with the officials like they do today.

My brothers and I just played hockey all day long every chance we got and we never expected anybody from the family to come. But one time – I guess it was a big game – I didn't know they were coming and my parents came. Wow! I don't even remember who won the game because what was important was that they were there.

I remember that.

A parish is a place where you come together and you really are important. You are royalty. You're part of God's family. You are called by name. Whether you're rich or poor, or whether you've been pretty good or pretty bad lately, you are special.

That's what a parish is. It's the only place in the world where everyone is important, really important. You feel that you're worth a million bucks or more.

Twenty-fifth Sunday in Ordinary Time/B cycle; Mk 9:30-37.

'You don't understand'

I remember one time, when my youngest sister (we have nine children in the family and she was the youngest) was in high school, and she was having a disagreement with my mother. As people that age tend to say, she said, "You're so old-fashioned. You don't understand . . ."

My mother sighed and said, "Well, that completes it. You're the ninth one to tell me that. So I feel a lot better."

I can picture coming in prayer to God and saying, "These things that we're supposed to believe and this way that we're supposed to live – it doesn't fit the modern world. People are laughing at us. This talk of peace, justice, this business about life, abortion – it's silly. It just doesn't work!"

And God would say, "Well, you're the 200th generation to tell me that."

Thirteenth Sunday in Ordinary Time/B cycle; Mk 5:21-43.

God at the center

I have only one relative left in Saginaw – my nephew Dan. The rest of his family has moved far and wide.

He got married a few years back, and I remember when they had their first baby. I was like the grandfather, because no other relatives were here.

And I watched what happened.

When a couple has the first baby, they give up a lot. It costs a lot of money. You're no longer going to take the kind of vacations you could have taken as just a couple.

Before that baby was born, I could call Dan and say, "How about some golf this afternoon?" He'd say, "Sure."

Now he sometimes says, "Well, I'm taking care of Trisha."

That baby was the center of their lives and their whole lives changed. I watched it. It was a wonderful thing to see. Why, it affected everything. A day at work was different for them, because of that baby.

They had to move everything aside to place the baby at the center, and yet everything else was lifted up by it.

So it is with God when we place God at the center.

Seventeenth Sunday in Ordinary Time/A cycle; installation of Fr. Don Dueweke as pastor of St. Patrick Parish in Croswell and St. John Parish in Peck; July 25, 1999; and installation of Fr. Mason Vaughn as pastor of St. Christopher Parish in Bridgeport; July 24, 1999.

Commandment of love

I was sorting out some of my books, and I found one of my dad's old books.

I looked through it and found that he was using a Father's Day card as a bookmark. Actually, it was a Grandfather's Day card. It must have been a very old one because the signatures are those of little children. It is signed: "Tim, Meg, Sally, Dan." Tim's and Meg's signatures are printed in that large print that children use. Sally and Dan obviously had theirs signed by their mother.

I was thinking about that when a light went on in my head. The Gospel speaks of one commandment of love – two sides of the same coin: Love of God and love of neighbor. Our Lord says that this sums up everything.

I was thinking that love is all one thing. It is all one piece. The love that Tim had for his grandfather is the same gift of love he has today for his wife.

We make a mistake when we slice up love into different kinds of love. We make a mistake when we make too many distinctions, and we learn a great deal about love when we realize that it is all one. Once we realize this, we learn to draw upon the love of one person, in order to learn how to love others.

Because love is all one.

I remember learning something like that in the game of golf. I remember learning that the golf swing is basically the same swing, whether you are swinging the driver off the tee, or a 9-iron to the green. It's the same whether you are hitting a 2-iron or a 7-iron, and sometimes you can learn by the way you hit one club how to hit another. Sometimes you are having trouble with one or the other of your shots, and you try to draw upon the swing with your 5-iron, or your driver – whatever happens to be your steadiest and best swing.

The same is true with love.

We've all experienced genuine, true love in our lives. It may be our love for our parents, or a parent's love for their children.

We can draw upon that to learn how to love others, because Jesus told us that we are to love everyone. It is a mistake to distinguish and decide that we love our enemy differently than we love someone we truly cherish.

We may have a tougher time loving certain people, but it's meant to be the same love. Even though we're not good at it, we have to try to make it the same kind of love. Single people must love as the Lord commanded us. Married people must love the same way. All of us must love our enemies, our friends, everyone who is part of our loves. That is very hard to do and it is, as a matter of fact, our life's quest.

It is the commandment Jesus talked about the most often. But unless we acknowledge that it is all one love, we start to hedge and we start to "spiritualize" our love of others.

You want to know how to love your enemy? Think about the way you love your brother or sister or mother or father. That is how you must love your enemy.

We won't love them quite that well, but it is meant to be the same kind of love.

Thirtieth Sunday in Ordinary Time/A cycle; August 8, 1981; Mt 22:35-40.

Part II
*I was born and raised on an island
in the middle of the Detroit River . . .*

I was born and raised on an island ...

—∿—

Andrew Untener managed the canoe livery on Belle Isle, a recreational island in the middle of the Detroit River. Along with seven other families who worked there, the Unteners lived on the 982-acre island.

Ken grew up in a three-bedroom frame house next to the canoe rental shelter. It was located near the MacArthur Bridge, which connected the island to Detroit. After the house was torn down in the 1940s, the Unteners moved to a home along the beach, where they lived until 1958.

As a result of Detroit's bankruptcy in 2013, Belle Isle has now become a Michigan state park. But while Ken was growing up there, Detroit owned the island with its canals and elms and weeping willows. Belle Isle had few cars and roads. There were no mail or newspaper deliveries on the island, no grocery stores or gas stations, no Halloween trick-or-treating. When they needed groceries, Mr. and Mrs. Untener drove to a farmers market in downtown Detroit.

Yet the island wasn't sheltered from real life. The Unteners lived on the island when a racially-fueled riot broke out on Belle Isle on June 20, 1943. The family would also occasionally see police boats trolling the Detroit River for a reported suicide victim.

But the Untener kids thought Belle Isle was an idyllic refuge. During the winter, the frozen Detroit River and its numerous canals became an ice rink where they learned to skate. During the summer, they fished and swam in the river. Belle Isle provided a front-row seat for the annual Gold Cup Hydroplane Boat Races and for the Detroit Lions' pre-season football training.

"I grew up thinking every kid had his own island," Ken told a reporter on Belle Isle's 100th anniversary in 1979. "It was a lot of fun – you had all the water and field sports in the summer and in the winter there was skiing and skating.

"In the winter everything was very still and the deer would come out of the woods," he would relate. "I have beautiful memories of those peaceful long winters on the island.

"Even in the summertime a peaceful walk was always in reach. You could walk along the water or ride your bike, just enjoying the fresh air, the flowers and all the people that you recognized . . ."

In the mid-1950s, the family moved off the island when Mr. Untener was transferred to another position in the Parks and Recreation Department.

They were the last family to live on Belle Isle.

Our House on Belle Isle

Salt and light of the world

———————

I was born and raised and lived on an island in the middle of the Detroit River – Belle Isle.

Belle Isle is a park. My dad worked for the City of Detroit, and was in charge of the canoes. The caretaker had a house there, the only home I ever knew until I went to college.

Because of that, I learned a lot of sports. I became and still am, to some extent, a hockey player – that's where all the hockey was played. I'm grateful for the opportunity to still play hockey and be un-Christian for about an hour a week.

One of the sports I learned was handball because there was a handball court right near our house, where the best players in Detroit played. As a youngster, I was taught by the masters. Fifteen or 20 years ago, I switched to racquetball because that's what everybody plays now. It was not a hard switch because the same principles still apply, so I had a jumpstart on the racquetball players.

I still play a lot. One of my nephews lives in Saginaw. He's a fine athlete now in his later 20s, and I taught him racquetball. I used to give him a 10-point spot. Then he got better, and I kept trying to teach him everything I knew and we played even.

For the last couple of years we've been dead even, but he never beat me . . . never . . . because I had the psychological edge. In the crucial third game, when things got tight, I expected to win and he wasn't sure if he could. He never beat me . . . until last Sunday.

We played last Saturday and we had a very, very close match. I won but I could tell by the look in his eyes that there was something different.

He said, "Let's play tomorrow before the Super Bowl."

I said, "Fine."

We played, and he beat me – beat me pretty bad. His game was the same as it always was. It's just that he concentrated and he somehow caught on that he could win. I could tell from the way he strode around the court. I tried everything, but I couldn't beat him.

If you believe the words of the Gospel – "You are the salt of the earth . . . you are the light of the world . . . your light must shine before others, so that they may see your good works and give glory to God" . . . something happens to you. Something happens to me. We will take our life up several notches, just as my nephew took his racquetball up several notches.

Jesus didn't say, "You go out and *be* salt, *be* light to the world." Jesus didn't say, "I'm going to *regard* you as salt and as light and treat you kindly." That's not what he said. He said: "You *are* salt . . . you *are* light. You *are* worth more than words could tell. You have greatness within you. You have fire within you. You are made with the image of God embedded in your bones . . . you're *that* good.

To believe that will change the way you live. But we forget it.

In that game of racquetball, I was trying to get my nephew Dan to lose his concentration. Toward the start of the third game, I called a time out and said that my glove was bad and I had to get another glove. I took my sweet time – about 10 minutes – not because I was tired. No, we were about even on the tired scale. I was trying to break his concentration and I couldn't do it.

If we can believe that we are salt and light, that we are worthwhile, with the fire of greatness within us, it will change everything we do.

I think I should probably put those words on my mirror so when I shave in the morning, I would see, "You are the salt of the earth. You are the light of the world."

I've got to find a way to remember that better and not to break my concentration. Because I believe it's true, and when I remember it, everything is different.

My life goes up many, many notches.

Fifth Sunday in Ordinary Time/A cycle; February 6/7, 1993; Mt 5:13-16; St. Mary's University Parish in Mount Pleasant.

Partnership with God

O ne of the advantages of growing up on Belle Isle was the handball court.

Back then, that is where the best players in the city gathered. From the time I was 10 years old, I was tutored in handball by the very best.

My brother was, too. He was two years older than I. When we were in high school, with that kind of tutoring and the opportunity to play all we wanted, he and I used to play as partners and we could pretty much handle anyone around our age.

Being two years older, my brother had the edge on me. I could never beat him in singles, and when we played as partners, I always knew that he made the difference. I could hold my own on the right side, but it was his performance that could turn the game around. We played well together as a team, but it was his ability that gave us the edge. He later won the city championship in singles.

I was thinking about all that when reflecting on Nicodemus' midnight meeting with Jesus. Is it God who deserves the credit for the success in our lives? Or do we?

That question was hotly debated at the time of the Protestant Reformation. Protestants tended to emphasize the fact that it was all God's work. We can do nothing good on our own. "We are justified by faith alone."

The Catholic side of that argument emphasized the importance of our participation. We need God's help, but we have a very real part to play.

At different times, we tend to forget either end of the argument. At the present time, I think that the greatest danger is for us to forget about God's involvement. We take all the credit for our success . . . or we take all the blame for our failure.

It would have been a great mistake for me, when playing handball with my brother, to think I carried most of the game. I didn't. Of course, it would have also been a mistake for me to think that my part meant nothing.

It is somewhat the same with God. God is our partner in everything we do in this life – small or great. God has come to give us some help. God's help and our work are both important – although God's help is most important.

How much room is there for God as a partner in the things I do from day to day? I don't mean the crisis moments in my life. I mean the day-to-day things. As the Gospel reminds us, God has come to give us some help. Do I leave room for him?

The custom of saying the morning offering is not such a bad idea. Some people used to (and still do) place it on their bathroom mirror so that they would begin every day with that prayer.

The morning offering or its equivalent should be part of every day. We take too much on ourselves. God never intended it that way.

God said, "Without me, you can do nothing."

With God, we can do everything.

Fourth Sunday of Lent/B cycle.

Polar Bear Freddie

$\mathcal{H}$is name was Polar Bear Freddie.
He was an old Russian, and part of the group that played handball, swam, and hung around the beach of Belle Isle.

He was tough as nails. He even played handball in his bare feet on rough cement courts.

But what made Freddie different was his habit of swimming during the winter. He'd be all bundled up while chopping a hole in the ice. Then he'd go to his car, put on his bathing suit (and have a nip of vodka), stroll barefoot across the ice, jump into the freezing water, and splash around for a while. The rest of us just watched.

We saw him almost every day, and enjoyed his company. When he died several years later, the obituary was the first time any of us ever knew his last name. To us, he was just "Polar Bear Freddie," set apart by those winter swims.

The waters of baptism (even though they give us a new name, too) don't set us apart as much as those icy waters set Polar Bear Freddie apart.

Baptism is taken quite in stride today. It wasn't always.

Picture the scene at first-century Corinth when word got around that so-and-so was going to be baptized and become one of those "Christians." That was hardly taken in stride. It caused a stir, perhaps akin to the stir caused back in high school when word got around that so-and-so was going to the convent or seminary. It was a big step, a radical departure from normal life.

To see baptism that way, we have to understand the symbolism of water. Most people see baptism as a washing away of the stain of original sin. But if we see baptism for what it really is – a plunge into a whole new way of living – then we realize that to jump into that water is to come out a different person.

Think about what baptism is meant to express. The person goes underwater and disappears (i.e. dies to the normal way of living in this world), then comes up with a new kind of life that is both strange and beautiful, the adventuresome life described in the Sermon on the Mount.

Or, as another way to look at baptism, the person crosses through water from one side to the other. They leave behind the regular way of living (in the ceremony they even leave their clothes behind) and cross over to a new way of living called "Christian."

It's a lot like Polar Bear Freddie. When he jumped into that icy water, he knew that it made him different from the rest of us, and that he'd be dubbed "strange" by most people.

There are a lot of Catholics who are gradually beginning to feel out of step with their country. It's catching many by surprise because it happened almost imperceptibly, like crossing a state line without noticing the signs along the highway. We're out of step, and people don't seem to be flocking to support our point of view.

If Polar Bear Freddie had ever gotten down because people weren't flocking to jump into the ice waters with him, I would have said, "Fred, I don't know how to tell you this, but I don't think this is going to catch on with most folks. Don't feel bad. It just isn't the sort of thing that's *likely* to catch on. It's what you might call 'different.' But the summer is coming, and then we'll all go swimming with you."

It is my lot in life as a Christian to be different. Our symbol is the cross . . . not a Gallup Poll. If people just watch us without joining in, or maybe even laugh at us sometimes – well, that's the way it is when you jump into this baptismal water.

All I can do is do my best in this strange sort of swim, and some day the Lord is coming to set it right.

And then it will be summer, and we'll all swim together.

Advent 1984.

Island lookout

We lived on an island. On Saturdays, my parents would often go to the farmers market in downtown Detroit to buy food in large quantities at good prices. Before leaving, they gave us our Saturday chores and we were told to have them done when they returned.

As soon as they left, we would have a great time playing baseball or whatever. When we figured it was about time for them to return, someone was posted along the shore with a pair of binoculars. They were the lookout and their job was to watch the distant bridge to spot the family car heading home.

It took about 10 minutes from the bridge. The moment the lookout sounded the alarm, we swung into action. No youngsters ever worked harder than we did during those final 10 minutes. We were never finished when they arrived, but we made a good show of making it look as though our labors had taken several hours.

That is one way to get ready for an arrival. You scramble to get things ready when you find out that the time is near. I used to think it was a pretty good analogy for a deathbed conversion. It was not what you call the true Advent spirit.

What is the Advent spirit? How does the Church get ready for the Lord's coming?

The disciples thought the best way was to know exactly when the Lord's coming would take place: "Tell us, when will all this occur? What will be the sign of your coming and the end of the world?"

Jesus told them that no one knows the exact day and hour. There are no binoculars to spot it from a distance, despite occasional fundamentalist claims to the contrary.

After squelching that idea, Jesus taught the disciples how to get ready: Simply make sure, day in and day out, that the poor and suffering are the center of your concern.

That was no casual remark on Jesus' part. It was the grand finale of all his teaching in Matthew's Gospel: "When the Son of Man comes in his glory . . . all the nations will be assembled before him . . ." He divides them into two groups and tells them that the whole thing is based on how they treated him in the person of the hungry, the thirsty, the stranger, the naked, the ill, the imprisoned.

This was no parable or allegory. It's the bottom line: If you didn't serve these people, you didn't serve him because he is in them.

We're not simply talking good works here. We're talking real presence.

Remember how Jesus identified himself with the leaders of his community? "He who hears you hears me." The stunning truth is that he identified himself just as closely with the poor and suffering: "As often as you did it for one of them, you did it for *me.*" Such works are not reckoned as *though* they were done to him. They *were* done to him.

Imagine. The Lord has the same identification with the poor and suffering as with Peter and the other apostles. The only way the Church can live up to its calling and get ready for the coming of the Lord is to respond day in and day out with his coming in the poor and suffering.

In the parish where I grew up there was a poor box. But it was small, and it was in the back corner of the Church. We had a fine St. Vincent de Paul Society, but they were only a handful of men. We had an occasional collection for the relief of war victims and others, but we didn't give away a regular percentage of our Sunday collection.

How does the Church get ready for the Lord's coming?

Not by scrambling to include some efforts for the poor among all the other things we are doing. Rather, by recognizing his special presence in the needy and suffering, just as truly as I recognize his special presence in the pregnant, young, poor girl named Mary.

There is no other way, says the Lord, to get ready.

Advent 1984.

The long-distance swimmer

I grew up on the water and I learned how to swim very early in life. By the time I was in high school, I had learned how to swim a long distance. I wasn't an especially fast swimmer in a sprint, but there was a fellow around by the name of "Sharkey" (it's the only name I ever knew him by. They said he used to fight sharks – probably a legend), who used to swim around Belle Isle (which is about seven miles by water). He got arrested a few times doing it because you're not supposed to be out there with the freighters. He showed me how you do the long-distance swim. He showed me how you lie in the water, totally relaxed. He showed me how you let your arms fall instead of moving them. He taught me a lot of tricks about how to breathe.

A couple of us used to go for some long swims – best on a rainy day when the water's calm.

One thing we did learn. Sharkey (although he didn't follow this himself) said you never go alone. So we'd always look for someone who liked to do a long-distance swim.

I remember what it was like – the two of you swimming for a couple of hours. You were trying to see how far you could go so you could talk about it when you got back. You weren't fooling around or anything like that . . . just the rhythm of swimming.

You didn't talk – you can't talk when you're swimming with your face in the water like you can when you're jogging. We never said a word, but you always kind of looked to see if they were there, and they looked to see if you were there. There was something about being together.

That has always been a special image to me. The person was there just to be there, and you were there with them just to be there. There are lots of different kinds of swimming – swimming in a pool with lots of people around, or learning to prepare for a race with the coach yelling things into the water – lots of different kinds of swimming. But long-distance swimming with that other person has a special meaning for me because I did it a lot.

Life is a lot like a long-distance swim, and, hopefully, we always have a couple of people who will go the distance with us, through thick and thin, when we're pretty good and when we're not so good.

The Lord is one of those people, alongside of us, every step of the way, just there to be alongside and to help.

Baccalaureate Address at Nouvel Catholic Central High School in Saginaw; May 1987.

Being home

One of the welcome results of my going around from parish to parish has been a gradual feeling of "being home."

I can't tell you what a good feeling it is to go to parishes and see familiar faces. To tell the truth, I thought I was giving that up when I was placed in charge of a whole diocese. I'm glad I was wrong.

By the providence of God, our lives are somehow brought together, linked, connected. We are put on the same road with one another, just as the Good Samaritan was put on the same road with the man in need.

I am always helped along by reflecting on my own human experiences. One of the helpful experiences in my life has been a family gathering during the Christmas season. We are a large family, and when we were all grown up and had pretty much gone our separate ways, we began making it a point to get together every Christmas and have one grand family party. Of course, we were family all year round, but coming together at the Christmas party helped to strengthen those ties and remind us that we were one family.

Parishes in the diocesan family need to strengthen and express the same ties. As with any large family, we have to be careful not to go off on our own and completely forget one another.

I can think of an experience from another part of my life. When I golf, I have a tendency (as many golfers do) of moving upward with my shoulders as I am hitting the ball. I guess I'm unconsciously trying to get the ball up in the air. I know that's not the way to do it, but it keeps coming back. A good golfer once told me that it's a natural tendency for someone of my build – whatever that means!

At any rate, it's something I always have to work against.

In the same way, I think that one of the natural tendencies every parish has to work against is the tendency to turn inward. Parishes, with all the good will in the world, can do this. It's not that we are selfish or anti-social. It's just an unconscious tendency we have to work against all the time. We have to keep reminding ourselves that we are members of a larger family of 105 parishes.

Another of my experiences, again from the world of sports, has to do with a rowing crew. When I was 15 years old, I was asked to be the coxswain of one of those eight-oared rowing crews. My job was to steer the boat and act for the crew like a jockey does for a horse. We had a great crew that year – we traveled all over and never lost a race.

One of the things I used to do was spend the first quarter mile or so just trying to get them rowing together. They were very good, and I knew that once they started swinging along together, no one could beat them.

But the secret was working together. I didn't want the starboard side letting the port side pull them around. I didn't want any of the oars hitting the water early or late. I wanted them all cracking together and pulling evenly . . . and if they did that, no one could beat them. And no one did.

My hope is that we can strengthen the bonds that make all of us part of the same "crew" – or better yet, the same family. We are a large family of many parishes, each with its own individuality, joys and sorrows. We need to pull together, pray for one another, enjoy one another, help one another, stay in close communion with one another.

Taped message to parishes; April 17/18, 1982.

What is it that is in me to be?

———————

When I was growing up, I lived near some woods. There were deer in the woods, lots of them.

I loved the time of the year when the snow was deep. My brother and I would head for the woods and watch for deer. The deer seemed so full of life. They were fast and could leap high and bound over fallen trees. Their fur was shiny and colorful. Their eyes glistened. On Saturdays, we'd spend all day in the woods.

There was also a zoo nearby, the Belle Isle Children's Zoo. There were deer at the zoo, behind the fence. They looked different. Their fur was scraggy. They didn't run or bound. Their eyes didn't glisten.

It's like winning a $25 million lotto and never having to work, just enjoying living off investments. Well, that's sort of what these deer had. They lived in luxury. They didn't have to hunt for food. It was given to them every day, and plenty of it. There was even a shed where they could go when it was cold and snowing. They had zookeepers who were paid to take care of them

But this isn't what these deer were meant to be. They were made to run fast and leap high, to feed off bushes and trees, to take some risks and fend for themselves in the woods.

What is it that is in me to be? Whatever it is, it was put there by God. When we have the courage to discover that, then we live life to the full, then we accomplish something good for all the world because God put each of us here to do that.

It may not make us famous.

It may or may not make us rich.

It may be difficult – like it can be difficult for a deer in the woods. But it is what is in me to be.

Don't look for the easy way. Don't take someone else's way.

It's like that slogan: "Be all you can be."

Religious Education Mass at SS. Peter & Paul Parish in Saginaw; Lk 10:1-9; January 26, 1999.

Walking on water

I've been trying to think about what it's like to walk on water. For example, I wonder if you get your feet wet when you walk on water?

Is it as though the waves become like marble and you step right across this hard surface? Or is it like walking through a puddle which, of course, we all did as children?

I grew up on Belle Isle. We always started playing hockey before you were supposed to start skating on the ice because we wanted to get out there and we knew when the ice would hold us.

So I'm an expert on walking on thin ice, and if I were to tell someone how to walk on thin ice, just to get across the canal, I would say something like this:

A couple of things you have to do. First of all, take a big step off the land because the weakest part is always along the shore because that's where the warmth comes from. Then when you walk, kind of drag your feet – don't take big clomping steps – but keep moving because you'll hear the ice cracking and you'll see it sagging and water will ooze out, but don't get afraid. Just keep moving.

If I gave someone those instructions, I can imagine them panicking (like St. Peter did) toward the middle of the canal, because it's cracking and it's going deep and there's water. Then they would either stop (in which case they would go through the ice) or they would start to run (in which case they would go through). I might reach out my hand and grab them and say, "Why didn't you trust me? All you had to do was keep moving at a steady pace. Don't worry about the cracking and the sagging and the oozing of the water."

Well, that's how I picture the scene of Peter on the water. Jesus said, "Now just keep walking," and Peter didn't trust him just as someone might not trust me saying that it was going to work.

It seems to me that's the kind of doubt and weak faith that we struggle with the most – the practical hesitation.

I don't think we have big problems with theoretical doubts about great doctrines and mysteries and so forth. Those are hard to figure out, but I don't think that bothers us as much.

I think there is a practical hesitation, a reluctance to do what we really know we ought to do. It's to keep moving in a certain direction, trusting that the Lord will see us through it, trusting that the Lord is there to reach out with his hand when it's too much for us.

I can think in my own life how at times it's that practical reluctance to move in a certain direction. It's not that I doubt the existence of God. It's not that I doubt life after death. I guess it's that I doubt that the Lord will see me through it. It's the biggest struggle that we face as we try to really trust that the Lord is here, leading us through.

That's what Peter faced, and I think that's why the early Church treasured this story, this strange story, because in a picture, it describes the biggest struggle we face as we try to really trust that the Lord is here, leading us through.

As difficult as it sometimes is, the Lord will see us through.

Nineteenth Sunday in Ordinary Time/A cycle; Mt 14:22-23.

Pearl of great price

Many years before I was born, and for years after I had grown up and left home to study for the priesthood, my family lived on Belle Isle. I have many memories of living on that island.

In the winter, when the west wind blew and blew hard, my brother and I used to go treasure hunting. The west wind would force water up stream and the water level would go down so that you could walk out 10 or 20 feet on dry land where the water used to be.

My brother and I would dress warmly and go walking along that extended shoreline, especially where people had been swimming. We always dreamed of finding an expensive diamond ring or some valuable coin.

We never found the diamond ring and we never got rich. We found some trinkets and some nickels and dimes, but we kept looking.

Everyone dreams of finding a buried treasure. Children read *Treasure Island*. Adults dream of winning the lottery. I guess people have always dreamed of buried treasure.

In the Gospel of the buried treasure and the pearl of great price, Jesus is teaching two things: To follow in his footsteps is not easy – we have to pay a price; and, in the end, it really is worth it to pay that price.

To follow the footsteps of Jesus is to pay a price. Let no one think that being a Christian means doing what comes naturally or doing one's own thing. It's not.

Jesus told his followers many, many times that it would be difficult. He said, "I wish it wasn't so, but there is sin within you and in this world, and to do what I am asking you to do is not going to be easy. You will suffer inside and outside. People will call you fools. But, believe me, I am teaching you to be the kind of person you were made to be, and the kind of person down deep you really want to be. But it is costly."

The thing is, most of us would want to pay that price all at once.

I remember when I was confirmed in the fifth grade, Bishop

Stephen Woznicki [an auxiliary bishop in the Detroit Archdiocese before he became bishop of Saginaw] called on me and asked me a question, as they used to do.

He said, "If someone told you that they would shoot you unless you stayed away from Mass on Sunday, what would you do?"

I replied bravely, "I'd tell them to shoot me."

Well, no one has ever threatened to kill me if I went to Mass. I never had a chance to pay the price in one swoop. But it has killed me a hundred times to say I am sorry. It has killed me a thousand times to bite my lip and not say things I wanted to say. It has killed me to forgive my enemies, to care about other people who don't really deserve to be cared about.

That is paying the price.

Day by day we pay the price in small change. It would be so much easier to pay it all at once, in one swoop. Jesus told us we would have to pay a price, that it would not be easy. But he also told us that it is worth it.

The Gospel story of the buried treasure is a true story . . . not just a dream. It has never come true for any of us, and we can't expect it to come true in our lifetime. But in following the teachings of Jesus, we are following a map toward a buried treasure. The treasure waiting for us is not some pile of merit.

The treasure is us.

Jesus is saying that if we follow his example and hear his teachings and walk in his footsteps, we will be a jewel. We will be a treasure to ourselves and for everyone else. We will be more loving than we ever dreamed possible. We will have a peace that the world cannot give. We will have a joy that no one can take from us. We will become the kind of person we always wanted to be . . . and the person we were made to be.

That is the buried treasure, the pearl of great price that is worth every ounce of suffering and pain that we pay out day by day in trying to follow Jesus.

Seventeenth Sunday in Ordinary Time/A cycle.

Part III

*Things I've learned about life
from playing sports . . .*

Things I learned about life from playing sports . . .

—ɯ—

Growing up on Belle Isle, Ken swam, played hockey, and rowed competitively.

As the team's smallest guy, "I used to be the coxswain of a New York rowing crew," he told an interviewer from Gonzaga University in 1993. "You know, he is like the jockey on the horse. In a race, I learned something. Don't use the rudder unless you absolutely have to because you slow things down. If the boat needs course correction, get them to row harder on the other side. A coxswain who is too rudder happy will never win a race."

Ken played sports, despite a congenitally deformed ankle that left his right leg shorter than the other. His leg would be amputated below the knee after he broke the ankle while playing handball at the seminary in his 20s.

"A deformed leg was socially awkward," he once said. "A wooden leg was not – you can kid about it. But the experience of my deformed leg was more valuable to me. I think I know what it's like to be the only woman in a room of men, or the only black among whites – I know what it's like to be noticed. I've been made sensitive to that."

In high school, he played goalie before goalies had to wear protective facemasks in hockey. After his ordination in 1963, he played hockey Thursday nights in the Detroit area with a group of laymen and priests (and a bishop, Tom Gumbleton). When Ken moved to Saginaw, he joined an over-40 Men's Slo-Puck league so that he could "be un-Christian for an hour."

Coincidentally, his 1980 ordination as bishop was held at the Saginaw Civic Center on the Saginaw Gears hockey team's ice rink. As he remarked about his mother during the ceremony, "This is the longest one of her sons has been on a hockey rink without throwing a punch."

As bishop, Ken often practiced golf early in the morning, sliding an envelope with his greens fee under the door of the pro shop. He inaugurated the annual Saginaw-Detroit Priests Golf Competition, held every summer in northern Michigan.

His nephew Dan lived in Saginaw, and the uncle and nephew would play racquetball on the courts at Nouvel Catholic Central High School (located in the same building as the diocesan offices). Ken also practiced with Nouvel's hockey team, and faithfully attended at least one football game every year at the University of Notre Dame. He was an avid fan of all sports and a fierce competitor.

And he especially loved the Detroit Red Wings, reminiscing about attending Wings games as a kid with his brother down at the old Olympia Stadium in Detroit. As a priest in Detroit, Ken became friends with the Red Wings' team doctor, and got to know several players and coaches. In 1997, he was behind the team's bench when the Wings won the Stanley Cup – their first since 1955, breaking the longest drought (42 years) in the league at that time.

For him, the lessons he learned from sports carried over into his life and his faith: "It's like a three-foot putt on the 18th green and it's all up to you. Someday, we're going to be standing before the Lord that way. It's going to be just you and the Lord."

Looking for the key

I enjoy playing sports and play a lot of different sports, and have been playing a lot of different sports for a long time.

I always look for the key that will make me better in a particular sport. There's always a key or a couple of keys because so many things happen, for example, in a golf swing that you can't think of all of them. So you look for the key. What is it – simple – that makes everything else happen?

The same thing is true in racquetball. I play a lot of racquetball. There are a couple of keys to win at racquetball – if I do them, then everything else happens.

When it comes to being just a plain, good person, I always look for the key.

There are different keys. It came to me as I was thinking of the people I have known, people who have been part of my life (some who have died). You know the kind of person I'm talking about. They were just good.

They were good, and the measure of their goodness isn't always the stuff we usually think of. My Uncle Julius was a great guy. We loved him. He didn't go to church much, and I guess there are some people just that way. He drank too much, and there are some people just that way. But, golly, he was good, and did we love him.

One of the biggest keys to being good is this: I am going to come down on the side of the people who are in pain. Now you say to yourself: That doesn't sound so brilliant. Somebody's hurting on the street . . . I'm going to help them.

A good person is someone who just about always is going to come down on the side of whoever's hurting. Let me tell you when that gets hard. No country in the world is built on that principle. I think we have a great country, but we killed people on the "other side" because we were right, and when you're right, you can hurt people.

The Church can act that way. A family can act that way, too. Organizations act that way.

Sometimes people are hurting because it's their own darn fault. People are in prison right now, hurting . . . and it's their own darn fault. But there's something in the good person that always comes down on the side of the person hurting.

Now I don't mean that everything they did was right. Good people just come down on the side of the person that's hurting, and they feel bad for them. They think that maybe there is something to be said – something on their side . . . not everything, but *something* on their side.

That's the measure. That's the key, and that's where the Gospel is coming from:

Blest are the poor. Blest are those who mourn.

Blest are the meek. Blest are the merciful.

Blest are the people who are persecuted.

Jesus came down on the side of sinners and rotten people who were hurting. He always did it.

I think it's the key.

Feast of All Saints 1990; All Saints Central High School in Bay City; Mt 5:1-12.

Get over it . . .

F rom 1963 until 1980 (the year I came to Saginaw), every Thursday night – winter, spring, summer, and fall – a group of us played hockey.

It was the same group and represented an interesting mixture of people – two of my brothers, some priests, and some people who had been on our hockey teams in earlier years.

One team wore red jerseys and the other wore blue, and the teams were the same every Thursday night. We may as well have been playing for the world championship because no two teams ever played harder to win a hockey game.

Now it sometimes happens in hockey that a minor fracas breaks out. This is because you move much faster on skates, and the resulting collisions are a bit more brutal. It also happens because in hockey, it's legal to roam around and knock other people down. Little injustices – at least *perceived* injustices – can build up in the course of a game, and suddenly flare up between two of the players.

That can present a problem because it interrupts the game. If those flare-ups start to happen regularly, you end up paying for an hour's worth of ice time and spending a good part of it watching two people fight.

In the course of our years together, we developed a way of dealing with that problem. We had a rule which, though unwritten, was clear to everyone. The rule was this: If it happens that tempers reach the breaking point, get over it and get over it fast.

In practice, it worked this way: We would break up the skirmish and tell the two players involved to get off the ice so that we could play hockey. Then we would make sure that they got over it before next Thursday night.

This was not only an expectation. It was a requirement. You see, if they didn't, then it would ruin the next game, and carry over to the next one too, and spiral ever upward.

Usually, it was resolved in the dressing room right afterward by someone cracking a joke about it and making sure that everyone had it in proper perspective.

Sometimes it was dealt with over a couple of pitchers of beer afterward.

There were occasions when it was a bit more complicated.

One example I recall was the time I more or less hit my brother over the head with a hockey stick. That was complicated for two reasons. First of all, by a stroke of bad luck, he wasn't wearing a helmet that night. Second, and a worse stroke of luck, his wife happened to be at the game that night.

She seemed to take it a lot more personally than he did. But I knew the requirement and so did he, and even though we couldn't resolve it simply by joking about it in the dressing room or over a pitcher of beer, during the week we worked it out.

We just plain got over it, and got over it fast.

It could have gone the other way. I could have pointed out to him that he had given me a pretty good elbow right in the chops a few minutes earlier and that contributed to the stick over the head. But that sort of thing goes on and on.

He could have brought up the time I tripped him before that, which is why I got the elbow, and I could have cited the time he slammed me into the boards.

That path never works. You simply swallow hard and get over it, and get over it fast.

Jesus gave us a way of dealing with hostility that is very different from the way of the world. He taught it. He required it of his community, and he lived it himself. On the cross he said, in effect, "I will not continue the spiral of violence. It all ends here."

We are all called to this way of life. It's not always an easy way, and there is no escape into abstract piety. It involved the hard, human reality of getting over it, and getting over it fast. You can never keep score or even the score. You just swallow it and the spiral of violence stops with you.

When we had those problems at our Thursday night hockey game, we didn't say to those involved, "Oh, please try to get over it. Do what you can."

No. It was a mandate. They had to get over it and get over it fast, or they couldn't be part of what we were about.

Installation of Sr. Patricia Wilson, SC, as pastoral administrator at St. John the Baptist Parish in Carrollton; Wednesday, July 25, 1990, feast of St. James the Apostle; 2 Cor 4:7-15; Mt 20:20-28.

Just pay up

Most everybody knows that I play hockey.
I've been playing hockey for nearly 40 years.

A group of us used to play almost every Thursday night at 11 p.m. year round.

I was the one who got the group together and I made all the arrangements to rent the ice rink. Ice time is not cheap, by the way. Ice rinks a while back cost $20 an hour; now it's $80 or $100 an hour.

When we finished our game or our practice and were sitting in the dressing room taking off our skates, I would look around the room, count up the number of players, calculate the cost, and then announce something like, "It'll be $5 apiece tonight."

There was a tradition – a routine – that they would always say, "Five dollars!" like it was outrageous. It reminded me of those predictable things on the "Honeymooners" or (going way back) on "Fibber McGee and Molly." At any rate, the guys would get out their money, and I would go around and collect it. Then I would pay the attendant at the ice rink.

If one of the players happened to be a young fellow in college or, occasionally, someone out of work, we always charged him less and the rest of us made up for it. We worked it out.

The whole thing was quite simple. We pitched in together to pay the cost. The money didn't go into my pocket or to some mysterious complicated financial network. We simply paid for what we had used together.

The next week we started from scratch and did the same thing.

I suppose someone could have said, "Look, I don't see why I have to do this. After all, I have to pay for my own equipment – these skates cost a lot of money (and they do). And there are gloves, and the shin guards, and the hockey stick and the tape."

True. But beyond the individual cost, there was the cost of what we did together.

Well, the Catholic Service Appeal [the annual fund drive for the Diocese of Saginaw] is really that simple.

Each year, I look around and figure out how much money we need to pay for the things we do together as a diocese, and divide it up. It doesn't go into my pocket or into some huge reserve fund or some complicated financial network.

It simply pays for the services we all use together.

1989 Catholic Services Appeal tape for parishes.

Expectation of others

*I*t can happen that others don't expect much of us.

It can happen that, instead of living up to high expectations, we end up "living down" to low expectations. That sometimes happens to youngsters who sense that their parents don't really expect much of them, and they end up – instead of *living up* to high expectations, *living down* to low expectations.

Well, here's my thought about the expectation of others.

Scotty Bowman coached the Detroit Red Wings to three Stanley Cups and is recognized as the best coach ever in the National Hockey League. I always wondered what he said in the dressing room between periods, especially if it was a big game and the Wings were down by a goal or two.

Did he rant and rave?

Did he give a pep talk?

I once had a chance to ask one of the Red Wings about that. What he told me was interesting.

He said, "Between periods, it was all business . . . no 'rah rah' stuff. Scotty would talk about our strategy, and he would make some adjustments and lay out the plans for the next period. That was it. But sometimes, after he finished and we were talking among ourselves, he might come over to one of us and say, not in a loud voice, 'I expect a little more of you this next period.'

"Let me tell you . . . when he said that, first of all, you knew he had confidence in you, and thought that you had it in you to lift the whole team to a new level. Second, you realized that you could rise to a higher level, and you'd go out there for the next period and play some of the best hockey you ever played in your life."

Now, I don't mean to compare Scotty Bowman to God (although some might think of him that way), but there's a lesson here. We can call one another to higher expectations. We can even call *ourselves* to higher expectations. But that's not all.

What if the Lord said that to me, "Ken, I expect a little more out of you"?

What if the Lord said that to us? Imagine the Lord addressing us by name, and saying, "I expect a little more out of you."

We'd be honored to think that the Lord had that kind of confidence in us. What's more, the Lord would add one more phrase. He'd say, "And I'll be with you to help you do it."

That's what Scotty Bowman *couldn't* do – he couldn't go out on the ice and help a player do better.

It's a prayer. Hear the Lord speak our name and then say, "I expect a little more out of you . . . and I'll help you do it."

Talk about a prayer that makes a difference! Try it. *I'm* going to try it this week. And you know what I think? I think it will be one of the best prayers we ever said.

Seventeenth Sunday in Ordinary Time/B cycle; Jn 6:1-15; July 27, 2003.

Stanley Cup

---

*I*t was June 7, 1997 . . . Joe Louis Arena in Detroit . . . fourth game of the finals of the Stanley Cup playoffs. The Red Wings had won the first three games against the Philadelphia Flyers. All we needed was one more game, and the Stanley Cup was ours.

The Stanley Cup.

The Red Wings hadn't won it in 42 years. Over half of the 16,000 people in the arena that night weren't even alive back when we last won the Cup. Along the way, there'd been some bad seasons – not even making the playoffs – and some mediocre seasons, and some good seasons.

But the Wings never managed to win the Cup, and people wondered if they ever would. Some teams have never won it in their entire history.

Now here we were, one game away. It was a close game, as were all three of the previous games. The Wings had scored a goal in the first period, and another in the second period. Now it was the middle of the third and final period – 10 minutes to go in the game, and we had a 2-0 lead.

The crowd was going wild. But it was nervous excitement. You could tell that everyone was hoping against hope that the Wings could hang on. Philadelphia was a very good team and could score two goals in two minutes.

Then the most astounding thing happened.

Down below the arena, at the back door, out of sight of any of us, National Hockey League officials were carrying the Stanley Cup into the building, anticipating that the Red Wings were going to win.

The TV cameras picked this up. Some people in the crowd had those small TVs, and they saw this and started passing the word around: "The Cup is in the building!"

Word started going through the crowd like wild fire. You could hear people passing it on: "The Cup is in the building." Within 60 seconds, everyone in the arena knew, and you could feel an electricity that I could not describe for you.

It was more than expecting to be able to look at the Cup. You could go to the Hockey Hall of Fame in Toronto and see it any time. What caught you was the fact that the Cup was here in *our* building, in *our* city, ready to be presented to *us*.

But it was more than that, too. It was the surge of confidence that this brought to everyone in Joe Louis Arena. Forget those doubts. We *are* going to win this. They brought the Cup into the building because they think we're going to win it. And we *are* going to win it.

And we did.

The world had been waiting a long, long time for a Savior, a Messiah. The human race had been trying forever to build a better world – with no more poverty, no more wars, justice for all. But we just couldn't do it. Some thought it would never come, and just couldn't be done. Many gave up hope.

And then, there came into this world, through an obscure back door – the small town of Bethlehem way over in the Middle East – the Savior, the Messiah, who was *God*.

The word started to spread. Angels went to shepherds in the fields and said, "Do not be afraid; for behold, I proclaim to you good news of great joy that will be for all the people. For today in the City of David a Savior has been born for you who is Messiah and Lord."

This was much more than believing in a God who is "up there," looking on from a distance. This was different. God came to stay. God is in the world, *my* world. God is here with us, for us.

But it was even more than just knowing God was here. It was the surge of confidence that this brought. We can build a better world. It's not just a dream. God believes in us, even more strongly than we believe in God. And, by God, we're going to do what we had begun to think we'd never be able to do.

We're going to win this thing, because *God is in the world*. After all those years of waiting, wondering, doubting, giving up hope . . . God is in the world!

Christmas 2002; Lk 2:1-14.

Importance of a connection

***

When I was a youngster in Detroit, my brother and I used to go down to Olympia Stadium to the hockey game and buy standing-room tickets. Then we'd wait until about 10 minutes into the game, and we'd look for some empty seats down there in the expensive seat section. We'd sneak down past the ushers and sit there.

A lot of times that worked. But sometimes it didn't because those people with the expensive seats would come waltzing in late and find these two little guys in their seats and would call the usher and "Out!"

Consider the difference when you have connections.

A few months ago, the doctor for the Detroit Red Wings called. I happen to know him, and he said, "You haven't been to a Red Wing game for a while. They're really good this year and they're playing Edmonton with the Great Gretzky. Why don't you come down and I'll fix it up and you can sit with me behind the bench?"

I said, "I think I can work that out."

We were going to have dinner at the Olympia Club at Joe Louis Arena (people who belong to this club can do that). I showed up and they wouldn't let me in because I didn't have a suit coat on. So I said, "I'm here as a guest of Dr. Finley."

"Oh, well, we'll find you a suit coat."

They found me a brown one that went real well with my blue pants and then, of course, we went to the bench. He said, "Well, maybe you'd like to meet some of the fellows before the game." So we went down underneath to the dressing room. A guy stopped me and I said, "I'm with Dr. Finley."

"Go right on in."

I talked to Coach Jacques Demers, gave him a few tips, and enjoyed the game immensely. What a difference it is when you have a connection.

Everyone could tell a story of how things like that have happened for them. You have a relative or somebody you know who has a connection and gets you into the theater for free through a back door or whatever. What a difference. You become more important than you really are if you have a connection.

Our connection with God makes all the difference in the world for us. What a difference it makes. Because of this connection with God, it doesn't matter if life seems useless because it never is. Everybody sometimes feels useless. It may be because you're sick and you can't do what you want to do. But every breath you take is precious because of this connection. Every pain you suffer is valuable because of your connection.

You may feel useless because you're old, or you may feel useless because you're young (teenagers feel useless a lot – unwanted, awkward). Because of your connection with God, there never needs be a moment when you're useless or when life is senseless.

Whether you are old or young, rich or poor, fat or skinny, whether you are doing well or doing poorly, we are connected to God.

Fifth Sunday of Easter/B cycle; Jn 15:1-8; St. Maria Goretti Parish in Bay City; May 1, 1988.

Just being present

God is everywhere and you can experience God anywhere. But when we come together at church and when we have symbols (stained-glass windows are great symbols), something happens or can happen.

The reason why we have church buildings is not because God isn't in our car, or God isn't in our house and we can't experience God there. But in church, something can happen that is a more powerful experience.

For example, the Detroit Red Wings won the Stanley Cup this past year.

I was there for the last game. The doctor who has been the team doctor for 40 years is an old friend. I sat with him behind the bench. (By the way, I learned some new words!)

I can't tell you what it was like in those last 15 minutes when, ahead 2-0 . . . we're 15 minutes away from the Cup we've dreamed of . . . the electricity in the air . . . the roar of the crowd!

The whole experience was more than what was going on down on the ice. It was more than what was taking place right there. We were all waiting for this moment for so long and you think it's near, and it was.

I could have been home in Saginaw and saved myself that long drive and watched that game alone on television. But it wouldn't compare to being there.

That's why we have church buildings, and that's why we want the richest symbols, and we want the best music. That's why we want people who just put their hearts into this because it is an experience of God. It is the Lord present in folks like us and in this world.

Talking about the experience and thinking about it alone will never do.

Second Sunday of Advent/C cycle; Lk 3:1-6; St. Mary's University Parish in Mt. Pleasant; December 6-7, 1997.

Doing great things

$\mathcal{B}$ack in the days of the greatest Red Wing players (Sid Abel, Ted Lindsay, Gordie Howe), I got to know Ted Lindsay a little bit.

Back then, the Wings had a terrific rivalry with Toronto. There were only six teams in the league. The rivalry was strong with all of them, but with Toronto it was fierce.

I remember Ted Lindsay saying to me one time, "We'd play Toronto for nothing. They don't have to pay us for playing Toronto. We'd play them for nothing!"

I was thinking, there are lots of things we do that we either don't get paid for, or things that we might get paid for but we would do them for nothing.

As I was reflecting on this, an astounding realization came over me. My mother is 88 years old. She had nine children. From 1922 to the present, my mother has never been paid one time, ever, for anything she did.

Think about that. Think of all the things that people do day in and day out that are not done for money.

Think about our own life. Think about the big things and the little things that we don't do for money. Those are the greatest things that people do. Those are the measure of a great life, and those are the things that the Lord holds precious. Those are the things that endure.

We tend to think that the things that receive the most money are the most important, the most valuable, and the things that require the greatest skill. One might think of a heart surgeon, for example, or someone who has a genius for business and does well. Or someone who is good with computers or investments.

If we erase money entirely from the picture and begin to look at the things that we do that are of value, the whole picture shifts. Furthermore, we begin to appreciate that great things are within reach of all of us. It doesn't matter whether you are a little child, or an elderly person, or a teenager, or educated, or rich. These are the most important, valuable things that anyone could do – and they are within our reach.

Sometimes we think that only people like Steven Jobs or the president do great things.

Not true.

Their actions may not even begin to measure up to the value of many of the things that we do, or things we could do.

Fourth Sunday of Easter/B cycle; Jn 10:11-18; Confirmation at St. John Vianney Parish in Saginaw, St. Hedwig Parish in Bay City and St. Paul the Apostle Parish in Ithaca; April 24, 1988.

Music helps us pray

---

*A*l Watrous from Detroit was big on the professional golf tour in the 1930s and 1940s. He was thought to know more about the golf swing than most anyone.

But Al never gave lessons. He enjoyed playing, not teaching.

One year, a fellow pro was having big problems with his game. He called Al and asked if he would help him with his swing for just a couple hours.

Al said okay, and the fellow took the next train to Detroit.

Al had him hit golf balls for about an hour, and he just watched. Finally Al said, "I have some advice. Remember this: What moves, moves."

The fellow thought about it, began to hit balls again, and all of a sudden, had his old swing back. He thanked Al profusely, got back on the train, and did fine the rest of the year.

A close friend of Al Watrous told me this story. I asked him, "But what did that mean: 'What moves, moves'?"

He said, "I didn't have the nerve to ask him."

Well, I have some advice that may sound similar. Remember this at every liturgy: When you pray, pray.

There is a difference between saying a prayer (or listening to a prayer) and praying. For example, when someone gives the invocation at a public occasion, often they do not seem to be deep in prayer. Their words seem directed more to us than to God.

My advice: When you pray, pray. Really pray.

To apply this to liturgy: Liturgy, pure and simple, is praying together. Everything we do at liturgy is to help one another tune in to God's presence and action.

Music helps us do that. It is a means to an end, not an end in itself. The criterion for any and all music at liturgy is this: Does it help us pray?

Sometimes, this fundamental purpose is easily forgotten. In planning a wedding liturgy, a couple might simply see four or five slots where a song can be sung, and proceed to pick out some favorites, without any regard for the appropriateness of the music. That's not the same as: How can we use music to help us pray during this liturgy?

During Mass, we sing at eight or nine points throughout the celebration. For instance, we sing after the first Scripture reading. Why? Not because this is where we are supposed to sing a song, but rather it is because this is where we pray. We sit back and think prayerful thoughts about the Scripture we just heard, and we do it by singing Scripture itself. That musical text is always from Scripture, usually the Psalms. We sing a refrain and listen to the choir or a cantor sing the text. It is a wonderful way to pray.

Each musical piece at liturgy has a purpose of prayer. Sometimes it is a prayer of praise, "Now Thank We All Our God" or "How Great Thou Art." Sometimes it is a prayer of petition, "Lord, Send Out Your Spirit."

Our reflective prayer can be greatly helped by a song sung by the choir after Communion, or by instrumental music during the preparation of gifts.

Golfers try to have a "swing thought" – one simple focus that helps all the complexities of the swing fit together. I have a couple of "song thoughts" that can help us pray better when we sing:

When singing a hymn at Mass, consider the text and ask: To whom am I singing? The answer will vary, and it helps to be conscious of the difference. For example, "Come Holy Ghost," "Precious Lord," and "Holy God We Praise Thy Name" are sung directly to God. To realize that one is singing to God can make a difference. "Christ the Lord is Risen Today" and "Morning Has Broken" are songs we sing out to one another, somewhat in the same spirit as we sing the "National Anthem" at some public event. We sing with more feeling if we notice to whom we are singing.

Where do these words come from? Very often they are taken from Scripture, e.g., "My Shepherd is the Lord." To know that one is singing Scripture can have an effect. At other times we are singing a text from the Mass itself – the "Holy, Holy," or the "Lamb of God."

Why are we singing? The gathering song, for example, is primarily to unify the assembly, pick us up and lift us into prayer.

It all comes down to where we started: At liturgy, when you pray, pray.

Seasons, Saginaw diocesan publication (summer 1996).

The right direction

A month or so ago, I played golf with a fellow who last year was honored as the best golfer in Michigan for the past decade.

He shot four under par. Don't ask what I shot. I wanted to shoot myself. He was a fine person, and we simply enjoyed the round of golf. He didn't try to correct my swing or anything like that.

But afterward, as we were having a sandwich, I said to him, "I noticed that as you stood over the ball ready to make your swing, you would always look down the fairway for four or five seconds. You'd stare at something out there, then you'd look down at the ball and start your swing. What is it you were doing?"

He said, "What I do is look at exactly where I want the ball to go. You see, your body is something like a computer. You decide where you want the ball to go and then your body makes it go there."

I told him, "You've got a different kind of body than I've got."

He said, "No, you have to work on your golf swing on the driving range – learn how to make the ball fade or draw, and develop a good swing. But when you're out on the golf course playing, you can't think of all those mechanics. I try not to think of anything except where I want the ball to go, and then let my body do it. This doesn't mean that it will happen every time, but if you concentrate on where you want the ball to go, it sets everything in the right direction and a lot of good things happen."

It struck me much later that this is why we pray.

We turn ourselves toward God, and when we do that, it sets everything in the right direction and a lot of good things happen.

It's not hard to pray. It's very simple, and actually we like to pray. That's not the problem. The problem is trying to do it from time to time when we're in the middle of our day. We forget to turn toward God. As a matter of fact, it doesn't seem that God "belongs" in the regular stuff of our day. God doesn't "fit" there – when we're caught in traffic, or in a meeting, or doing the things we do all day.

That's what's hard about prayer. That's what Jesus talks about in the Gospel – being persistent in our prayer, sustaining our prayer.

When we manage to do that, it sets us in the right direction, and a lot of good things happen.

Twenty-ninth Sunday in Ordinary Time/C cycle; October 21, 2001.

Personal prayer

---

*I*n golf, when I miss a putt and still have perhaps a three- or four-footer left, I am often tempted to step up and finish it off, rather than wait for the others to putt.

But I learned the hard way that I tend to hurry those kinds of putts when I am out of turn or I am too distracted. So I established the principle that I will always mark my ball and let the others putt.

That is a principle. I no longer have to decide in each case what I want to do – even though, in some cases, I am very tempted to get it over with. This principle is solid enough so that I consistently do not do it.

What important principles are operative in my life?

For example, do I have principles about forgiveness? Jesus spoke a lot about forgiveness. Do I simply forgive when and where I feel like it, or do I have some basic principles about that, principles that will overcome my feelings in individual instances?

Do I have principles, for example, about talking negatively about people when they are not present? Jesus had a lot to say about that, too – about kindness – and I wonder what principles, if any, I have built into my life about kindness.

There is also the question of generosity. Jesus spoke a lot about that. Do I simply give when and where I feel like it? Or do I have a principle about generosity, perhaps a percentage of my income?

Do I have any principles about prayer? I was thinking, wouldn't it be nice if I had? Just a small example – a principle that I would never eat food without first saying a prayer of thanks to God, at least privately. I don't have that principle in my life and, just as an example, it would be a good one.

I know that I need principles in my life. This is a personal opinion, but I think we have moved away from principles. I am not saying that everything has to be based on operative principles so that our life is rigid. But we do need some, and I question whether people today have many.

I'm not even thinking of whether or not they have the right or wrong principles – I'm thinking about whether or not they have *any* principles. We seemed to have moved into an "I feel" kind of morality. We try to do what we feel would be the best in different situations.

Well, I can't trust my feelings that way. I need principles, and I think that the wisdom of the ages proves the need for principles.

Ninth Sunday in Ordinary Time/A Cycle; Mt 7:21-27.

Bear Archery strike

It must have been 30 years ago when Bear Archery in Grayling, Michigan, had a strike.

Now I don't know a lot about it, but I used to spend my summers as a counselor at a boys' camp up in that area. I knew Grayling as a sleepy little town. I also knew Bear Archery as the best place in the country to get a bow and arrow. It wasn't a great big industry, but it was a skilled local industry that provided jobs for many people.

There was a strike, and it was a long strike. After a while, Bear Archery offered the jobs to other townspeople. Some of them took the jobs, and some of those who had been on strike went back to work.

It split the town right in two. Neighbors, family members who were on opposite sides of that issue wouldn't talk to one another.

I remember reading about it and seeing some things on television about it. A family member would be sitting in a restaurant having a cup of coffee and someone else would walk in (perhaps a cousin or in-law who was on the other side), and he would walk right out. They couldn't even talk to one another.

We could probably tell stories of issues that split families and towns like that. I don't want division. But sometimes, if you believe what the Lord says, and if you try to live it and you try to speak it, there will be division.

I don't like that.

I want my Church to be made up of sleepy little churches out there in the country, everybody smiling and the towns delighted to have them there. But it can't always be that way. When you speak the Gospel and you speak about the poor and you speak about war and you speak about social structures, it causes division sometimes. And it's hard.

I guess I have to ask myself if we're willing not to seek division but to live the Gospel and speak the Gospel, *even* when it comes out that there's going to be some trouble. The temptation is always to waffle.

Jesus was honest. He could have said, "Sometimes even this nice guy from Nazareth is going to get a reaction that's going to split people and families and towns." It takes a lot of courage.

I have to ask myself – we all have to ask ourselves if we, individually, and if our parishes as a community are willing to go with the Gospel, even when those kinds of things happen.

Twentieth Sunday in Ordinary Time/C cycle; Lk 12:49-53.

Part IV
I've been a priest for many years . . .

I've been a priest for many years . . .

—〽—

Like many high school students, Ken wasn't sure what he wanted to do with his life after graduation.

He knew he didn't need to "climb the ladder" to be happy . . . and he knew he wanted to "be free" and to do something that could make a difference.

In the winter of 1955, during his senior year at St. Charles High School in Detroit, Ken decided to become a priest. He entered Detroit's Sacred Heart Seminary College, and later studied theology at St. John's Provincial Seminary in the Detroit suburb of Plymouth. Ken was ordained June 1, 1963, by then Archbishop John F. Dearden for the Detroit Archdiocese. The Second Vatican Council began the previous October, and Archbishop Dearden would play a key role at the historic council, particularly in the writing of the document, *Gaudium et Spes (Pastoral Constitution on the Church in the Modern World)*.

"No group in 1,500 years has experienced the change experienced by my ordination class," Ken told an interviewer. Before his ordination as deacon in 1962, he had asked the smartest faculty member at the seminary whether he should purchase his breviary in Latin or English. The professor assured him the breviary would always be in Latin, no matter what the changes. Two years after Ken's ordination, the breviary was changed to English.

The new priest was assigned as one of four assistant pastors at St. Mary's of Redford Parish, a large northwest Detroit parish with a grade school and a high school. Within two years, he was given a chancery post – first as assistant chancellor, and then three years later, as assistant vicar for parishes.

From 1969 to 1971, Ken was sent to the Pontifical Gregorian University in Rome to obtain his doctorate in theology. The experience was life-changing for him, as he immersed himself in the center of theological thinking. His doctoral thesis focused on a major

Vatican II figure: "The Church-World Relationship According to the Writings of Yves Congar." Doctorate in hand, Ken became the assistant to the archdiocesan Delegate for the Clergy and, in 1975, was asked to teach homiletics at St. John's Seminary. In 1977, he was appointed St. John's rector – the youngest priest ever named to the post and the first St. John's alumnus to become its rector.

In October 1980, Cardinal Dearden summoned the 43-year-old Untener to his office for a closed door meeting. The cardinal told him he was to become bishop of the 11-county Diocese of Saginaw, located in mid-Michigan.

Ken knew that his name had often been rumored as a future auxiliary bishop. But that had never happened. He was surprised to hear that now he would become a bishop with his own diocese. Ken was reluctant to become bishop, asking himself, "Can I do this and still be myself?" After much prayer, he accepted the appointment.

Ken often said he expected to live out his priesthood as the pastor of a parish. But God had other plans.

"I tell myself, 'Ken, don't try to gauge or measure how it is that God is working through you," he said in 1995. "Just do it. It's only measured from a distance, usually a distance long after I'm dead."

Why I decided to become a priest

W hat I have to say about my decision to become an ordained priest, or my feelings about this life, may come as a surprise. At first it may not seem dramatic enough. Believe me, it comes from the depths.

In late high school I knew that I wanted to do something with my life. The trouble was, I didn't know what. All I knew was that I didn't want it to be "normal." I wanted two things: To be free (what high school youngster doesn't!), and to make a difference.

It began to dawn on me (I don't remember how) that being a parish priest held out (for me) the widest possible freedom (speaking, writing, celebrating, helping, connecting), and a chance to make a difference (dealing with people at times of birth, death, marriage, boredom, crises, everyday stuff, and more besides).

But there was more. Being a parish priest meant that I could settle into what I wanted to do, without having to race toward something else. Now that was a big thing for me, and it still is. I need to explain.

Not long ago, I came upon a television news clip about a fellow in a small Nebraska town who made violins, cellos, and violas. He was fairly young, and somehow had acquired this craft. It was his life's work.

The story fascinated me, for in a way it was my own. You see, this young man had a woodshop, and he crafted these musical instruments.

It takes a long time to make a masterly-crafted cello, or violin, or viola. You have to select good wood, with tone and beauty. Then you have to shape it, carve it, sculpt it into a musical instrument. There was no machine to do the shaping. It was all by hand. But it was more than just the shape. It was the sound.

Now this fellow did this as his life's work. He wasn't looking over his shoulder to something else. He was doing what he wanted to do. And what he did was helping people to make beautiful music, for people came from all over the world to buy his violins, or cellos, or violas.

Expansion? Branch offices? Upward mobility? Promotions? Big bucks? These were the furthest things from his mind. He was doing what he wanted to do, and what he did was something beautiful for God and for people. He could settle into what he wanted to do, and what he was good at, and not have to worry about all the things that people often worry about.

The story of what he was doing was so different from the driving force of "expansions" or "mobility" that seems to come at people because of social pressures. There are subtle drives that come at us from all sides. Families and friends watch to see if you are moving upward, grabbing opportunities for improvement, higher salaries. They watch the car you drive, the house you live in, the clothes you wear.

You may like the line of work you are in but then . . . people seem to expect you to move upward. We live, after all, in an expanding economy. You are expected to get promoted, to have a larger and larger office, a higher and higher salary, better perks . . . and it all shows up for all the world to see in the car you drive, the house you live in, the clothes you wear.

If you have a craft, well, then you're supposed to expand, open up some branch offices, be alert to every possibility of growth . . . relocate if you have to in order to take a whole new job that opens up, but be sure it's a step upward, and then be ready to do it again in a few years . . . and on and on it goes.

To see this fellow settled into making cellos and violins and violas was so, so different. The peacefulness and joy on his face, the feeling of doing something worthwhile, something that helped others make beautiful music . . . it was almost too good to be true.

When I saw this news clip, I realized that it was a metaphor for what I was about.

I can craft homilies and articles, speak the right word to someone in need of a good word, celebrate liturgy, anoint the sick, prepare people for marriage, help people approach death as a good friend, speak the good news of the Gospel . . . and settle into this art, this craft of being a parish priest . . . this life of doing something so good it was almost too good to be true. And to have no pressure to expand, to be alert to new opportunities . . . no pressure to look over your shoulder to something else – the only pressure is to do well what you do. You are in the thick of life, crafting words from the good Word of the Gospel for people who want only the right word to help them make their lives into music.

I honestly think that this is what drew me to this life. I did well in grade school and high school, and I knew I could at least try to go into any number of professions. But as I thought of each of them, they seemed to be on a track that could become a treadmill.

More than that, they didn't have enough "elbow room" . . . horizons wide enough to let me be creative, like the fellow making violins. I was drawn to parish priesthood because I saw a wonderful opportunity to write, and to speak, and to lead people in ritual, prayer . . . to wake up every morning and go to bed every night knowing that this is where I want to be, what I want to do . . . and to do nothing more than that.

This was the "workplace," the shop that I wanted. This was my home, the place from which I could do what I wanted to do.

This was freedom. Do you think that when I sat down to write this, I had a manual? It was like writing a song. It may be good, or not so good. I can simply try to write something good, and know it is good when people hear it and find it to be helpful.

I don't mean to take away from other professions . . . but there is something so good about this one, and that is all I want to say. There is something good about every life lived for God – married, single, business, public service . . . I only wish to tell about this one, and say that I have found in it a home, a place to settle into and find fulfillment in using the talents that God gave me.

I think of the words of the beautiful Psalm: "O Lord, my allotted portion and my cup, you it is who hold fast my lot. For the measuring lines have fallen on pleasant sites; fair to me indeed is my inheritance." (Psalm 16:5-6)

Seasons, Saginaw diocesan publication (fall 1996).

The river trip

When I was in seminary college, I spent most of my summers as a counselor at a boys' camp up near Gaylord.

One of the things I was in charge of was taking the boys out on overnight canoe trips down the Au Sable or Manistee Rivers.

Another counselor and I often talked about taking a trip by ourselves, and doing it at night in order to enjoy the peaceful stillness of nature. After talking about it, we finally did it.

I have a couple of suggestions for anyone who is thinking about doing something like that.

First of all, it would probably be a good idea to pick a night when there is going to be a moon. We didn't, and it gets dark out there.

Second, you probably should decide beforehand who was supposed to bring the flashlight. As we were crawling around in the dark, we had a little discussion about that.

In the middle of the night, it started to rain so we pulled to the side and scrambled up the bank, found a level place, and managed to pitch our tent in the dark. In the morning, we were awakened by a truck. As it turned out, we had pitched our tent in the middle of a dirt road.

I thought about all that when I read the Gospel about the Temple coming down.

We build a lot of things that have to come down, or that fall down by themselves. It is difficult because usually we don't know the reason why it has to come down.

On my midnight trip, it was easy – a Mack truck a few feet away is fairly obvious. But most of the time, it is not easy, because we are still in the dark.

We all build a lot of temples. We make plans – not only life projects but plans for next week. We build temples because we feel our plans are good, even holy. There is no question that our intentions are good, so were the intentions of the Jews who built the Temple . . . but it had to come down.

People build temples for their children, and it is hard when those temples come down. We do it in reference to our friends, our families, ourselves, our plans at work. We build a lot of temples.

What we don't realize is that sometimes they really aren't for our own good or for the good of others – at least they aren't in the long run. They are right in the middle of the road that leads to God's kingdom.

We have to make plans and we have to build things, and that is good. But don't build temples. Don't make them so sacred that they would appear to have been built by God.

Think of that tent in the middle of the road.

Sometimes we are in the dark and we simply have to trust in God.

Third Sunday of Lent/B cycle; Jn 2:13-22.

Ken Untener

People who shaped my faith

I spent a good part of my life studying theology. After finishing parish grade school and high school, I went away to the seminary – four years of college seminary, four years of theology after that.

Then I was ordained a priest, and six years later I was sent off to Rome to get a doctorate in theology, with two years of classes over there and five years after that writing a doctoral dissertation.

And you know what? Do you know who has shaped my heart? You know who has nurtured my faith more than anyone else?

My mother and my dad . . . and some other people along the way who were regular folks, but who were just trying to do their best to love God and love their neighbor. People who tried to spin out in their own lives the story of the life of Jesus . . . who were members of this imperfect Church and who knew and loved its customs and traditions.

There is no question that they have touched my heart and shaped my faith more than anything.

I think back – we talk about the old days when I went to Catholic school for 12 years (a parish school) and the sisters and what a great job they did (and they did).

They never claimed to be theologians. They studied the subject they taught. They got degrees in English and history and math and it took them a long time to get those degrees because they had to study during the summer. Some of them were out at 20 years old, teaching. They did such a great job because they shared their faith. They never claimed to be sophisticated theologians. They just claimed to believe and put their lives on the line.

The same faith we all have.

Fifth Sunday in Ordinary Time/A cycle; February 3-4, 1990.

The cardinal's representative

When I was a young priest, I had a big job in the Detroit archdiocese.

I was really low on the scale, but I worked in the archdiocesan offices, and that's where everything was going on.

This was in the 1960s and early 1970s. There were all kinds of problems, and I was the guy who got sent by Cardinal John Dearden into one place or another where a parish was in turmoil for whatever reason, or where there was a personnel problem, or whatever.

I want to tell you something. To tell you the truth (it only dawned on me as I meditated on the Gospel reading about being sent out in the Lord's name), it's a lot easier to be sent out on behalf of somebody else than to go out and do it on your own.

You see, I was out there representing what Cardinal Dearden had said you have to do. I went into places where, to get near it, the police were directing traffic because it was so crowded. People were all waiting for this person whom they'd like to lynch.

You know what? It wasn't hard. I was representing someone, something. I wasn't really the one they wanted to lynch. As I looked back, I thought, "You know, it was easier to be sent out on behalf of someone – not that you had a script to follow. You had to think on your feet and had to be able to deal with stuff – but it was different." There was a sense of support and security, and you just did your best.

But it really struck me. If I could go into a day and realize what I believe to be true (sometimes it's easier to believe something than to realize it) that the Lord has sent me into each day. Not necessarily to solve problems or turmoil, but maybe to bring the Lord's love to the clerk in 7-Eleven.

I'm acting on behalf of God. None of us goes out on our own. We are the hands and the eyes and the mouth and the feet of Jesus Christ. I need to go into a day like this: "It's you and I, Lord. Here we go." I know it was easier and more effective when I knew I was going out on behalf of Cardinal Dearden.

But Cardinal Dearden ain't nothing compared to God.

If I realize that I'm going out on *God's* behalf to bring God's love to someone who never gets any attention, or to bring the hard truth to somebody that's going to have to hear it, it's very different.

Jesus had that sense constantly. *The Father has sent me.*

Missioning Mass; Jn 14:21-26; May 19, 2003.

The sing-along

---

*W*hen I was ordained a priest in 1963, it seemed that the emphasis was on what the Eucharist is and not as heavily on what it does. You have to emphasize both.

We have been trying to do that in recent years, and I think it's interesting. If I was giving somebody a tour of the cathedral, and I was going to talk about the Eucharist, I wouldn't take them over there to the Blessed Sacrament chapel. I'd bring them to the altar because the Eucharist is something that we *do* together.

There is interaction with all of us and with God, with the risen Lord, with the Spirit. This is where all of that happens. The Blessed Sacrament chapel is where we reserve for the sick and the dying what we have *done* here.

This shift in emphasis, or widened emphasis, has its effects on ordained priesthood. I frequently use the analogy of music. Thinking of God as music, the role that I thought I had in 1963 was more along the lines of the concert pianist who brought the music – brought *God* – to the people. Now, 34 years later, I see my role at Eucharist more like the sing-along pianist who is trying to connect with the music (God) in the people. That's quite a difference.

There are three things that I've learned from trying to play at sing-alongs and applied by analogy to priesthood.

The first is this: The sing-along pianist has to know music. If people want to sing this or that, and I keep saying, "I don't know that one," it's not going to go very far.

In the same way, the ordained priest who is going to lead the celebration of the mysteries of God has to know God . . . and know God very well. In this, you must imitate Jesus who was so close to Abba, God . . . so close that the crowds recognized a difference in the way he spoke. Like Jesus, you will have to spend a lot of time in prayer, even if sometimes you have to get up early to do it. You have to know God very well.

Second, you've got to know the people and love them.

A couple years ago, I was in Australia to give a priests' retreat, and one night they asked me to do a sing-along. Well, I loved them but I hardly knew them. I didn't know their songs and it didn't work. You can only do "Waltzing Matilda" so many times.

In this, a priest must imitate Jesus: "I know mine and mine know me." You must be close to the people, truly close.

Third, the thing about sing-along piano players – the good ones – is that they are never the center of attention. The music is the center of attention. Once you get it rolling, the people are enjoying their singing together so much that the piano player is just someone helping it happen.

The piano players could easily make themselves the center of attention, but then it's their show and the people lose a wonderful opportunity to experience the music that's in them.

Ordination of Steve Gavit; Jn 6:51-58; August 17, 1997.

Teaching preaching

---

*T*welve years after my ordination as a priest of Detroit, I was asked to teach preaching at St. John's Seminary in Plymouth.

I hadn't taken any advanced course in preaching. I simply had the regular preparation that all candidates for the priesthood receive.

So I prepared by talking to regular folks about homilies. I carried a "Colombo notebook" in my pocket (like the old TV detective, Lt. Colombo). Every chance I got, I'd ask people what they liked or didn't like about homilies. I wrote down what they said, sorted into categories, and that's what I taught.

I remember talking to one person who was in her 30s and had a fairly tough life. She was separated, was raising a couple of kids on her own, and worked as a nurse. I asked her what I should teach these priests-to-be about preaching.

She thought a few minutes and then said, "Tell them that you guys get to go on a retreat every year, and a day of recollection now and then, but the only 'retreat' I have is going to Mass on Sunday. Just once I'd like to leave Mass feeling better than when I walked in. Just once I'd like to feel consoled. I'd like to hear something that just makes me feel good, but usually I feel like I got bad marks."

I never forgot that.

It reminded me that what we celebrate at the Eucharist is good news. That's what the word "gospel" means – "good news."

Twenty-eighth Sunday in Ordinary Time/C cycle; October 14, 2001.

Answering Yes

When Cardinal Dearden told me that I was asked to be the bishop of Saginaw, I was honored to be asked but I began to tell him my limitations.

I started to suggest some others who ought to be considered first.

The cardinal interrupted me and said, "You aren't being asked *who* should be the bishop of Saginaw. You are being asked if *you* would be the bishop of Saginaw."

The way the question was put made all the difference in the world.

Each of us is being asked not *who* should be a disciple of the Lord, but if you would be his disciple.

We have answered "yes" many times, and ever since then this Church has been our home. We are a community of people mysteriously called to be here, called to this our home, by the Lord.

"Come Home" Advent tape, December 1984.

The bishop's motto

W hen I was serving as a priest in Detroit, all of a sudden I received word that I was to be appointed the bishop of Saginaw, and it was to happen soon.

I learned that there are some things you have to do, and one of them is to have a crest with a motto on it. My family didn't have a family crest, so I had to come up with a motto. A bishop usually chooses something from Scripture or something from our old tradition – just a couple of words.

It's hard to come up with a motto.

Imagine that you had to come up with a motto and you were to choose a couple of words from Scripture or from one of our old sayings that would somehow in your mind characterize the kind of Christian you want to be. What would you come up with? Well, it's hard.

But then all of a sudden I remembered – and it happened quickly – I remembered my favorite couple of words in all the Gospels. Jesus said, "I have come that they might have life, and have it more abundantly."

The reason why those words meant so much to me is because they are the opposite of what we often believe to be true, or sometimes even the opposite of the way the Church can act. Don't you sometimes get the impression that to join the Church is just the opposite of what Jesus said? Instead of coming out of the confinement of the sheepfold and into the wide open pasture, you join the Church and you get taken into the sheepfold, and you are more confined. There are things you can't do and it's more stifling of free thought.

Isn't it interesting that Jesus uses just the opposite image: "I have come to open the gate and to bring you out and to give you pasture. Thieves are just trying to slaughter, to destroy . . . I'm trying to give you life, to open up new freedom."

It's true.

We've all experienced times when things haven't been going well. You haven't been doing very well; you bring your sins to the Lord and you hear those sacramental words of forgiveness. That's one of the most freeing moments there is. You walk out feeling full of life.

When you belong to a believing community, there is a certain security in that and it gives you the freedom to question and not be frightened by doubts, and to tune into each other and our traditions and not to feel totally lost and at sea. You have the freedom to do that.

Belong to the community of the Lord's disciples. Dream great dreams – why, there is a vast destiny, no matter who you are – tiny crying children, old persons, sick persons who spend every day on their backs.

Your life has meaning every moment, for you are God's daughter, God's son. You have a vast destiny and you can dream great dreams of a life that never ends.

Fourth Sunday of Easter/A cycle; Jn 10:1-10; confirmation at St. Agnes Parish in Pinconning, St. Mary Parish in Nine Mile, St. Cecilia Parish in Clare, and Sacred Heart Parish in Mt. Pleasant.

Substance versus form

---

*I*n Mark's Gospel about the person expelling demons, the issue is between the substance of what is accomplished and the outward form.

The person who is expelling demons in the name of Jesus had bad form. He was using the wrong formula, and he also had the bad form not to belong explicitly to the disciples of Jesus.

On the other hand, he apparently had good substance. He believed in the God of Abraham, Isaac and Jacob. He believed in Jesus . . . and it should be pointed out that he probably believed in Jesus as much as the disciples did at that time. He believed in helping people and was trying to cure the sick (which is usually what is meant by "expelling demons").

When faced with the issue of substance versus form, Jesus usually emphasized substance. On one occasion, in a dispute over some of the purification laws, Jesus said that it is not what goes into people that counts, but what comes out of them – the substance. Of course, it was easy for him to do that. He never had to run a parish!

The more you try to make your vision a social reality, the more important form becomes. It doesn't become as important as substance. It simply becomes more important than it was before.

For example, if you are living alone, it is only the substance that is important – food, heat, light, and having a roof over your head. The schedule you keep, whether you do the dishes every day, whether you hang up your clothes – those things don't matter. But if you're living in a family or in some kind of a community, the form becomes much more important.

Substance versus form – the two are not unrelated. One affects the other. The ideal is to have good substance and good form. But of this you can be sure: Good substance can make up for bad form . . . but good form cannot make up for bad substance. The question is which one we emphasize or overemphasize. Which one needs development?

Many of the issues that have been argued about these past 25 years have had to do much more with form than with substance – whether to receive communion in the hand or on the tongue . . . whether those who help the priest at the altar should be boys or girls . . . whether the unleavened bread that we use for the celebration of the Eucharist can have a dash of salt in it or not . . .

I remember when I was ordained a bishop at the Saginaw Civic Center. One of the things I was concerned about just before Mass had to do with the phrase "all men" in the words of institution over the wine. It was in the phrase, "shed for you and all men."

At the time, some priests simply said, "for all" and this was causing some turmoil. That is the way I had been doing it, but now I was to say my first Mass before all the people of Saginaw, and before all the bishops of Michigan and Ohio and from other places.

I was wrestling with what to do.

I decided to stay with my practice of saying "for all."

When you look back on a thing like that, you get a perspective and realize much more the difference between form and substance.

In his opening speech at the Second Vatican Council, Pope John XXIII said, "The substance of the ancient doctrines of the Deposit of Faith is one thing, and the way in which it is presented is another."

He was distinguishing between substance and form, and he was reminding the bishops of the world that they had to address the need to change the form of many of our rituals, our ways of expressing and teaching doctrines, and so forth.

All of us in ministry have to think about that. Form is something that can be developed, but usually it can be developed only through some type of evaluation, review, continuing education, mentoring.

Perhaps we have felt that form wasn't all that important. However, it is bad form that makes some sermons flat and boring. It is bad form that makes a liturgy dull. It is bad form that makes the pastoral care of the sick less than effective. It is the bad form that makes people feel unwelcome in the community.

Twenty-sixth Sunday in Ordinary Time/B cycle; Mk 9:38-43, 45, 47-48; St. James Parish in Bay City; commissioning of lay ministers.

'I'll pray for you'

When I first came to the Diocese of Saginaw (I had been here a month or so), I was asked to go visit a hospital because there was someone there who was dying and wanted to see me.

So I went.

It was a woman in her mid-forties who was dying of cancer. She died a week or two after I saw her, but when I went to see her, she was sitting up in bed.

She said to me, "I wanted to meet you before I died, because when I found out about the cancer two or three months ago, it was about the same time that it was announced that you were going to become the bishop here. It's been very hard and it's been very painful.

"I've followed in the papers your coming, your ordination, and I just wanted you to know – I don't know why I did this – but I offered everything up for you, that you would be a good bishop."

Well, I tell you, you can imagine what an impact it had on me to hear her say that.

And she just wanted to tell me that.

There have been moments when I've been tired or whatever, and I would think of how she prayed for me, and it's always been a way of picking myself up.

Seventh Sunday of Easter/C cycle; Jn 17:20-26.

Boldness in ministry

---

*I*t takes a certain amount of boldness to be a minister. The other day I was talking to somebody at the *Detroit Free Press*. They had called to interview me and find out some of the ways in which the priesthood today might be different from the priesthood of yesterday.

After thinking about it for a few minutes, I suggested that the main difference was the fact that today's priest is called upon to exercise a kind of spiritual leadership that formerly we reserved for very special people.

In the past, priests were very dedicated and gave themselves to the service of their people by performing sacred tasks. Now we don't have as many sacred tasks that are reserved to us. We are spiritual leaders, and that can be scary. It takes a certain amount of boldness to step forward and be a spiritual leader.

The kind of boldness referred to in the Letter to the Hebrews is one that is freely exercised. That might be a little different from the kind of boldness I can have when I get angry. Then I am more under the power of impulse or compulsion. But to be free of that and still decide to do something as bold as being a spiritual leader – that is the kind of "boldness" referred to here.

I can remember when I lacked that boldness.

The first time I ever gave a talk to a group of priests was years ago at St. John's Seminary. I remember how uneasy I was, and my presentation was – as they say in tennis – tentative.

After the talk, some of the priests followed me out into the stairwell (I was trying to get away as fast as possible) and they said something like, "Look, we didn't ask you to do this because you are necessarily better than we are. And you don't have to be great to do this. It's just that somebody has to do it . . . so do it!"

I know that at other times in giving a homily where I notice that people from different areas of expertise are present, I hedge a bit and apologize, saying something like, "I'm not a Scripture scholar, but . . ." or "I'm not an historian, but . . ."

I should just get up there and do it.

Another time when I get tentative is the last blessing. I would much rather stand here and say, "May the blessings of God . . . come upon *us* and remain with *us* forever." Well, the people want somebody to bless them, and I should just stand there and bless them.

This kind of boldness is not the same as being dogmatic or rigid or authoritarian or dictatorial. The person who acts in that way really thinks (or tries to project) that he or she really is better. It doesn't take any boldness to act that way if you think you are better than someone else or present yourself as if you are. What requires boldness is knowing that you are no better, and that you have to stand there and do it anyway.

As I look back, some of the best things I could have done and didn't do were because of a lack of boldness. There sometimes are things, hard things I should say, and they really would be honest and I believe helpful. But I lack the boldness. I don't want to take on that role. Or there are times when I fail to introduce anything about the Lord because I don't want to appear to be "holier than thou." I lack the boldness.

It takes a certain amount of boldness to be a ministering person.

In the Gospel, Jesus talks about planting seeds. Maybe if I realized that all that I am doing is planting seeds, then I can be bold.

If someone told me to go out and build a maple tree, I would have to say that I don't know where to begin. I don't have the expertise to make a maple tree. But if someone told me to go out and plant a seed for a maple tree . . . well, I can do that.

Maybe that is what I need to appreciate in ministry. It is when I am humble and honest, and genuinely realize that what I am doing is the Lord's work, that what I am administering is the Lord's gifts – it is at those times that I can truly have the boldness it takes to be a ministering person.

Talk at St. John's Provincial Seminary; Letter to the Hebrews 10:32-29.

A priest quietly dies . . .

I was giving a priests' retreat in Milwaukee, and things were going fine.

Wednesday night (our last night together), we decided to have a bull session. Things got off to a lively start, and stayed that way until well after midnight. You can pretty much guess the issues that came up – the shortage of priests and whether celibacy was the cause, altar railings, kneelers, the pastoral letter on the economy, evaluations of priests, Catholic schools. Eventually we drifted off to our rooms one by one.

During the night, Fr. Bill died in his sleep.

He was 63 years old, and very much in the thick of the retreat. He seemed hale and hearty, was a lively fellow, and having been rector of the Milwaukee major seminary, was pretty well known by all of us.

No one knew he died.

The next morning, we had breakfast and then morning prayer. On our way to these events, we were walking back and forth past his room, unaware he was in there, dead.

At the closing conference, I talked about the issues we had discussed the night before. I pointed out that all these issues have to be seen in the larger context of the kingdom. We have to learn to "relativize" the issues (they were proud of me for using an "ize" word), I said. We need to look back and see the issues that were so important in grade school (I desperately wanted to be window pole boy in first grade), or in high school (the senior prom), or in the seminary (who was going to be head prefect), or when we were first ordained (saying the Latin canon of the Mass in an audible tone).

Looking back, we smile and realize that these were all relative.

Well, come the kingdom, the great issues in today's Church will be about the same. Make no mistake about it, they're important. But they're relative. The Lord smiles as we make them seem so absolute, much as we smile looking back to first grade.

While I was saying all this, unbeknownst to us, Fr. Bill was lying dead in his bed.

I went on. There are two ways to relativize. The first is not to care about anything, and that is the wrong way. The second is to be in touch with the great mystery of God, to experience firsthand the breadth and depth of the magnificent reality that lies at the heart of our lives and spreads out in a panorama that the whole universe cannot hold.

Altar railings? Economics? Issues, to be sure, but how they pale in the brilliant light of this great mystery.

I brought my talk to a close. "Dig in and work hard and try to build a better Church and a better world. But don't act as though each piece is part of a kit for building the kingdom. When the kingdom *does* come, most of our best accomplishments will be put aside, like a lot of the things we did in first grade. Scripture says: 'In the Lord's eyes, one day is as a thousand years and a thousand years are as a day.'"

We celebrated our closing Eucharist, then had lunch, and then we all went home (Fr. Bill was the only one who really went home). We still didn't know he had died. It was only the next day that someone found him dead in his bed.

Since then, when I give priests' retreats, I imagine one of the priests dead in his room. It makes me understand how relative it all is. The hierarchy, parishioners, religious superiors, ushers, musicians, liberals, conservatives – while we're wrestling with all the great issues, Fr. Bill is lying dead in his bed.

Advent 1984.

I'm a bishop

There's a difference between knowing something and really *knowing* something.

To use a trite example, I can remember very distinctly when I was three years old. Youngsters that age are taught how to answer a certain question because people always say, "How old are you, little boy?"

And so I was a child prodigy, and I could say, "Three."

It was automatic. I knew it.

Old Mr. Peterson fixed the canoes on Belle Isle. I wandered into his shop one day and he said, "How old are you?" And I said, "Three." Then it struck me. One, two, three – I'm brand new! A youngster just thinks they've been around forever. I realized – I can remember as distinctly as can be – *I am brand new!*

About 12 to 13 years ago, I was sitting in the cemetery at Sheridan Corners.

It was a summer day and the place was empty (actually, it was empty because I was an hour off from when I had to be there). I hadn't planned to go there and pray but there was nobody there, and there was nothing else to do.

I can remember this very vividly. You can see a long ways in any direction there. And there came upon me an awareness that I'm a bishop.

You can have that awareness, of course, and do the functions that a bishop does. You confirm and you ordain and you make decisions, and you do this liturgy.

But on that day in the cemetery, there sank deep within me an awareness that God wants to act through me. And I was called not to *do* stuff, but to *be* something for the people of Saginaw, to let the Lord act through me.

It was an overwhelming experience that I really can't adequately put into words, but I can tell you that for me, it's been different since then.

It was the difference between knowing my identity and *really knowing* that the Spirit of the Lord is upon me, and I am called to be holy, and I'm called to affirm the holiness of others.

It was – enough said – just very, very different.

Chrism Mass; Lk 4:16-21; April 15, 2003.

'Bridge' Time

1 just finished 15 years of being bishop of Saginaw. I have been bishop of Saginaw longer than Bishop (Francis) Reh was bishop, longer than Bishop (William) Murphy, the founding bishop. I have been bishop of a diocese longer than any of the seven bishops in Michigan. The millennium is approaching so you think these long thoughts about the Church – where are we going? About the world – where are we going?

I find it very helpful to accept and thank God that I am in the Church at this particular time in the Church's history. We are living at a "bridge" time. We are still building the bridge from something gone by to something yet to come. We're the bridge-builders. It's got its pluses and its minuses, but this is where God placed us, just as God placed Mary and Joseph where God placed them.

So I think it's helpful – I find it helpful personally – to thank God for putting me here in Saginaw and being part of this bridge-building. I think it also helps to remind myself that I probably will never see the results.

Great bridges take a long time to build. I probably won't live to see the results of what it is that we are all about – just as St. Joseph never lived to see the results of what he was participating in.

There is another thought that I find helpful. I say to myself, "Ken, leave something to God. Don't think that you are controlling the entire future."

I'm God's servant. I do my duty. God is the master builder and it helps to remind myself to leave something to God, for it is God who writes straight with crooked lines and who builds the future.

Which leads to my next inner reflection that God *does* write straight with crooked lines. God works from within history. God works with the ordinary things of life. And, strangely enough, God works even with our weaknesses – the weaknesses of us individually, as parishes, as a diocese, as a Church. God works through common things.

Lastly, because God works that way, I tell myself, "Ken, don't try to gauge or measure how it is that God is working through you. Just do it. It's only measured from a distance, usually a distance long after I'm dead. So, again, just as Mary and Joseph are good examples, do what it is that God has called us to do in this time in the world and the Church, and don't try to measure how much is being accomplished by God through me."

Those are my long thoughts and, as a kind of a footnote to all of it and through all of it, keep a sense of humor.

Comments at the end of Mass at St. Frances X. Cabrini Church in Vassar and St. Bernard Parish in Millington; December 3, 1995.

Tackling technology

---

*J*esus came to take the human race to a new level in its development. It wasn't a matter simply of touching up something here and there. It was a break-through, a dawn, a fresh, exhilarating, new level of human life.

He uses some images to show the difference between a break-through to a new horizon, and simply a touch-up of the old. Thus the images of trying to patch up an old sweater by tearing a piece out of a new sweater, or putting new wine into old wineskins.

Let's update the images.

When I learned how to use a computer some 15 years ago, the Write program I used was one of the early ones and, of course, it was not a Windows program. I got to know it very well. I could move texts around, take shortcuts, move blocks of material right to left and left to right. I could do it without thinking, and I could play it like a piano.

Then came Windows.

Well, I didn't shift to Windows right away. I stayed with my Write program and I could manage. I could go back and forth, although it took some work. In the earlier Windows programs, I could find ways to go back and forth to a non-Windows program, and set it up with my printer.

But the more Windows developed, the more difficult it has become. And now, in some cases, it is impossible. The printers being built right now don't take into account my primitive Write program. When I'm trying to pull a text down from the Internet, it won't go into my Write program.

The time has come when patch-ups won't work anymore. I've got to make a decision. I've got to let go of my program, change the software, and learn a new program.

It's so hard. I'm so good at the one I've got. I feel exactly like the kind of person Jesus talked about in Luke's Gospel: "No one who has been drinking old wine desires new, for they say, 'The old wine is better.'"

That's what I kept saying to myself: This program works better. Well, that's partly because I know it so well and am familiar with it. The truth is, it won't fit the new anymore than you can patch up an old sweater with a piece from a new one.

It's not as though the old is entirely thrown out. The hardware stays the same. There's the same technology in the computer. It's the software that changes, a whole new way of using this technology, a whole new way of using what's there in the computer.

Jesus came with a whole new way of seeing life. It was a breakthrough, and the breakthrough is still happening. It is still the dawn, the beginning.

But we have to catch hold of it because the old way of seeing things is still in all of us.

Opening Mass at Nouvel Catholic Central High School, Saginaw; Lk 5:33-39; September 4, 1998.

Scent of unforgiveness

Some time ago, I read a book about forgiveness written by a fellow named Lewis Smedes.

It was a revelation to me. I learned that forgiveness involves three steps.

First, I take some time to think about the person I need to forgive and, instead of totally identifying that person with whatever they did to hurt me, I begin to see them as a human being like me: An imperfect child of God. There's more to that person than whatever they did to me. What I tend to do is see the person *only* in terms of the problem between us, but that's a distortion. That person has a life and it involves the same things that are in my life. I need to put him or her in a larger perspective. That may seem obvious, but when we're hurt and angry, it's another story. This simple step can make a huge difference.

Second, I give up my "right" to get even (we really don't have a *right* to get even, but we think we do because "they've got it coming"). This second step gets at the heart of the word used in the Gospel – the word that means "to let go." Giving up the "right" to get even involves not only letting go of whatever vindictive things I was going to do in return, it also involves "letting go" of vengeful thoughts. Those thoughts don't make the other person suffer – the other person is totally unaffected by whatever vengeful thoughts I cook up. Such thoughts hurt only one person – me. They rot in my stomach and have a bad effect on me.

Third, I ask the Lord to be with me and, together with the Lord, I look at the other person. For sure, the Lord wants good things to happen to that person. So, with the Lord's help (and with some struggle) I look at that person the way the Lord does. I pray for the person and, with the Lord, I decide that I want good things to happen to them.

When I have taken those three steps, I have achieved forgiveness.

That takes care of the question of *how* we forgive, but *why* should we forgive?

There are a number of good reasons why we should forgive. For example, it brings healing and peace to our own lives. Nursing a grudge is bad for our health.

There is a prayer I like to say at the beginning of each day. I didn't write it myself. It's an old prayer and it goes like this:

O God, you created me and put me on earth for a purpose.

Jesus, you died for me and called me to help complete your work.

Holy Spirit, you inspire me to carry on the work for which I was created and called.

I have to ask myself each day whether I will bring light or darkness, goodness or evil into the world. I have to remind myself that God has created me and put me on earth for a purpose.

A few years ago, an appliance store owner gave me a small stand-up freezer with a door on the top that you lift open. He thought I could use it to keep a small supply of frozen food which I could microwave for lunch. I put it in the back room of my office. The truth is, I hardly ever used it.

One Christmas someone gave me a frozen turkey, and I put it in that freezer. Then I forgot about it. A year later, I got another frozen turkey, and I put that one in the freezer. That's when I noticed the turkey from the year before.

One night, the electricity in our building went out for a few minutes, but then came back on. I hadn't noticed this because everything was up and running the next morning. Trouble is (as I was later to discover), the freezer didn't restart when the electricity came back on.

About a week later, I came into the office very early in the morning to get a few things done, and as I was coming up the back stairs, I noticed a strange, foul smell in the air. I wondered what it was.

As I came nearer to my office, it grew stronger. I followed the odor and it took me to that back room off my office. It was coming from the freezer.

When I lifted open the top, it almost knocked me over. I won't give you the gross details of what I saw – and smelled – but I'm sure you can imagine it. I spent the next two hours emptying and cleaning the freezer, and spraying Lysol into the air, and lighting candles and doing everything I could do to get that smell out of the air.

And so back to the question: Why should I forgive?

When I think about that freezer, I see things differently. It's not a matter of, if I don't forgive, God will get me for it. No, I realize that to harbor vengeful thoughts and feelings in my heart, to have unforgiven baggage rotting within me, is like those two rotting turkeys in my freezer.

These thoughts and feelings give off fumes, and they flow into the world around me. I really can't keep them inside me, anymore than the door of that freezer could hold inside the smell of those rotting turkeys.

The question is: What do I want to flow from me into this world: The fragrance of God's love, which I am called to mediate into creation . . . or the stench of unforgiving thoughts and feelings that I have inside me and which inevitably flow into the world?

When I think of it that way, I see things differently. I would never want to radiate into the world the putrid fumes of vengeance. I realize that God created me and put me on earth for a purpose – to help bring God's love more fully into the world.

God's love for me, God's gracious forgiveness refreshes my soul, and I want to bring more of that into the world.

It's as simple as that.

Twenty-fourth Sunday in Ordinary Time/A cycle; Mt 18:21-35; September 15, 2002.

Week of Christian unity

---

*I*n January, when we traditionally pray for Christian unity, I become more aware of the tragedy of the split in our Christian family.

You know, there's nothing worse than a family fight. Memories last too long, and the worst turning point in a family fight, in a family split, is when you get used to it. You're used to not having them there at Christmas and Thanksgiving. You're used to not calling, writing, sending a birthday message.

We've gotten used to a family split in Christianity. We didn't cause the split (it goes back 450 years), and it's not our fault. But it is our responsibility as family to pray that we come back together as one. It is our responsibility to sense the pain and to be conscious of the tragedy of family division. There are people who should be here with us. They're not here, and we're used to that. It's too bad.

Tomorrow I am going to move from St. Stanislaus Parish in Bay City. I like to move. I always say I move as soon as my room gets dirty.

I'm going to move tomorrow to a different kind of place. Because it is the time of prayer for Christian unity, I'm going to move into the home of the Episcopal bishop in this part of Michigan.

I called him up about a week ago and I said, "Bill, I'm thinking that maybe we ought to live together for about a week and just say it in deeds, not just in words. If we can't share the same eucharistic table, at least we can share the same supper table."

He and I have met before. As a matter of fact, I went over there to dinner once, and so we know each other a little bit. And he said, "Ken, I think that's a fine idea. I think that's a great idea. I think that would do a lot. It would say a lot. It would be symbolic, and I think we ought to do it – just a minute while I go ask my wife!"

Fortunately, she said okay. So, tomorrow morning I'm going to move in and spend the week.

But it is a shame that we can't share the eucharistic table because the worst thing in a family fight is when you get used to it.

We've got to get together. The Lord can accomplish things that we can't accomplish, so put it in his hands.

It's the Lord's family, after all.

Third Sunday in Ordinary Time/A cycle; Mt 4:12-23.

What makes a great parish?

I wonder what makes a parish a great parish?
The things that make an organization great by Fortune 500 standards aren't necessarily the same things that make a parish great in the eyes of the Lord.

If we were going to use this world's measurements, a person might say, "This is a great parish, this parish I belong to, because it has an oil well and it doesn't cost us any money. Everything's free. It's got air conditioning, too, and we don't have to pay for it because we've got oil. And it's got thick carpet and great, comfortable cushions, and the priest looks like Robert Redford and he never preaches long – one minute and it's over with. And the buildings are magnificent . . ."

There's nothing wrong with a priest who looks like Robert Redford, and there is nothing wrong with having air conditioning. There is nothing wrong with having carpets and cushions on the seats. Nothing is wrong with a short sermon now and then.

But those aren't the things that make a parish great in the eyes of the Lord. If you think about it, what are some things, in no particular order, that make a parish truly great?

One thing is caring. A good parish is a place that you never have to deserve, that you never have to earn. People here can say to anybody, "I'm glad you're here." That would make it a great parish, even if they were in debt.

I go around to different parishes. At the parish I moved into the time before last (I move about every two months), there happened to be a phone in my bedroom. It rang about 5:30 in the morning, and woke me out of a sound sleep. I just grabbed it said, "Hello, this is St. *(where am I?)*. What parish are you calling?"

"St. John's."

That's it.

"St. John's, yes." I sure wasn't going to tell them who this is. "What can I do for you?"

They said, "I have a call here for the bishop."

I said, "Just a minute, I'll go get him!"

Anyway, I move every two to three months, and I can tell the spirit of a parish. When you move, you can tell the difference. I can't tell how you do that, but you can tell the difference.

It's the chemistry. There is life. People smile. People come toward you, not go away from you. You can tell by the youngsters in the sacristy. People laugh and look comfortable when they sit there. I can tell. There is a certain life, a certain spirit to a great parish.

A great parish not only cares for people but there is involvement. If you look at a parish and see how it spends its time and its money, you'll know what is important and if it is a parish that cares by doing something for people.

A great parish loves God (I wouldn't want to leave that out!). It's a parish where the word "God" comes easily to people's lips, and I guess that you could tell that partly by being in their homes. You could go from here to the domestic Church, and God would be in the air. There would be a picture, a statue, prayer before meals. That makes a parish great. Even if it doesn't have a $100,000 picture of Jesus, it has the rich treasure of Jesus being in the hearts of the people.

A great parish is inclusive. Everybody is always welcomed. At Tiger Stadium, everybody's welcomed in the bleachers. That's where my dad always took us because he didn't want to pay a lot of money for us to see a ballgame. There were too many of us. Everybody is welcome in the bleachers.

Want to go to the owner's suite? You have to wear a suit and tie, and not everybody gets in there. But in the bleachers, everybody is welcome. Somebody who is not usually welcome in places in this world could tell you in an instant what a great parish is if they can walk in and feel welcomed.

Another feature is money that goes outside the parish. Even though an individual isn't rich, there are people out there worse off than you are. A great parish is a parish that gives money away around the world.

Unity. A great parish has inclusiveness and different kinds of people and lives out what Jesus prayed, "That they may be one." Parishioners have a sense of being together, not like being at separate tables in a restaurant, or being anonymous people at a theater, but people who smile and are together.

Parish histories can never tell the greatness of the people who cared, who believed in God, who welcomed, who included people, who went out to people who were in need – in need of someone to talk to or in need of money or in need of food – and helped them.

. . . and nobody ever knew it.

Fifteenth Sunday in Ordinary Time/A cycle; Mt 13:1-23; 100th anniversary of St. Patrick Parish in Croswell; July 15, 1990.

Habitat House

---

*T*wo years ago I spent a day working on a Habitat House. It's no small thing to build a house, but you don't do it alone. People with all kinds of skills, and people with no skills join together in the project.

I showed up on the site and they must have had an intuition about my skills as a carpenter, plumber, or electrician because do you know what they assigned me to do?

Well, there was a truckload of dirt that had been dumped on the site, and they needed the pile of dirt moved by wheelbarrow from one part of the site to the other. My job was to stand there and shovel the dirt into wheelbarrows.

All day.

That's what I did – shovel dirt.

And you know what?

I enjoyed every minute of it.

Not that shoveling dirt is a barrel of laughs. I enjoyed it because I knew that I was part of this great project. I was helping to build a house for someone who didn't have a good house. I was helping to build a house in a neighborhood that was run down, and this would help to make that neighborhood a better place.

I enjoyed it also because I was doing this together with a lot of other people, and even though many of us had never met before, there was good spirit in the air.

Whatever your age and whatever the circumstances of your life (even if they seem meaningless and monotonous), we should know that we are part of something magnificent. If we bring to our day some goodness, if we bring to our day some light – if only through a smile – we are part of this colossal good work that is God's good work. We can know that it's more than just "shoveling dirt." We are sharing with the Lord and with his disciples around the world in building the kingdom of God.

The key to happiness and to a sense of fulfillment, whatever the circumstances of your life, is this: To know you're part of this great enterprise of God, and to enjoy being part of it.

Third Sunday in Ordinary Time/A cycle; Mt 4:12-23; January 27, 2002.

Why Mary is like good wine

---

*A*ll my life as a priest I lived in a parish until I was assigned to St. John's Seminary, and I was there for three-and-a-half years as rector before I came to Saginaw.

But all of my priesthood I spent living and working in a parish, although a lot of the time I also worked in the chancery office.

At one of the parishes I lived in, there was a fellow who was a connoisseur of wine, and he had his own wine-importing license. That is hard to get, I'm told. He could import wine directly from France. He had a lot of money, and he was a bachelor, and he liked good wine. He used to give wine to the rectory. He'd get a shipment of wine and he'd bring a crate over to us.

I knew nothing about wine. Zero. On Thanksgiving Day, my dad would splurge on Mogen David and we thought it was terrific.

Well, I'm living in this rectory and I was not there a lot for supper. But I'd come in at night late, and I'd want to have a snack. I'd get out a bologna sandwich and I'd see an open bottle of wine. So I'd take it and pour half a glass, and have a bologna sandwich and rare vintage French wine. Only I didn't know it was rare vintage French wine. I didn't know wine. But I lived there for several years, and I began to get used to drinking that kind of wine with my bologna sandwiches.

Then I went to Rome to study in 1969 for two years, and they served the table wine. I poured some wine, drank it, and said, "What is this – lighter fluid? This is terrible stuff."

It wasn't vintage wine, for which I had unknowingly cultivated a taste.

So I learned a little bit about wine. One of the things that this gentleman taught me was that you never drink good wine apart from food. There is an after-dinner wine, but it's more like a port wine. I had absorbed this by osmosis, but he explained that when you come in at night, at least have the bologna with it – don't just drink the wine by itself because it's cultivated to blend with the taste of food and the food brings out the taste of the wine. They're designed to go together. Great connoisseurs of wine only serve it with dinner because wine is meant to bring out the taste of the food, and the food brings out the taste of the wine.

I never realized how that's the way it's supposed to be done.

That also helps me understand that Mary is like good wine. The whole role of Mary in the Church is to go with the Lord Jesus, her son and whose disciple she became.

Mary is a magnificent assistance to us in bringing out the full-bodied richness of Jesus. When we think about her as his mother and what the implications of that are, and we think about her as his disciple and the implications of that, it helps us understand more about the Lord. It helps our relationship.

It's like good wine. But, like good wine and food, Mary is not meant to be separated from Jesus and discussed in isolation from him.

In the course of centuries, sometimes Jesus became a bit obscure for people because the accent on his divinity made him too distant. In some cases, people began to look to Mary herself, and felt more able to identify with her because she was not divine.

That's fine – identifying with Mary is a wonderful way of helping us journey through life – but not apart from Jesus.

In some ways, we then begin to treat Mary somewhat the way a person would if they took a bottle of good wine and drank it apart from the meal.

It's like taking good wine out of context.

National Conference of Catholic Women Convention; May 5, 1982.

What's the use?

The hardest thing that I have to do is visit homes for the aged. I do a lot more of that as a bishop than I did as a priest, because when I'm staying in a parish they want me to visit the old people.

And I do . . . and it's hard for me. But I grit my teeth and I know it's the right thing to do and I do it.

One of the reasons it's hard is because it takes a long time and it doesn't seem to accomplish very much. A lot of the people don't even know I was there. A lot of them don't know who I am. Sometimes you just take their hand and say an Our Father, and sometimes you get a squeeze back, and that helps to make it worthwhile.

But it's hard.

When you leave, you wonder what you accomplished. That also characterizes some of the other hard parts of my ministry. I guess I would characterize my temptation by the question: "What's the use?"

It's the same question I hear a lot of people asking, "What's the use?"

I hear people asking it when talking about the issue of nuclear arms: "What's the use? We don't have the power to control it."

I hear people asking it in the context of the economy: "What's the use? We spin our wheels. The movers and doers are the ones who control the economy. What's the use?"

I hear people ask it in terms of poverty and hunger throughout the world. You bring up some canned goods at the presentation of gifts at Mass, but, really, in terms of this world, in terms of an impact, what's the use?

I hear people ask it, trying to raise families: "What's the use? They get out there in the drug culture and everything that I tried to instill seems to evaporate. What's the use?"

You know, it does make you wonder – what did Jesus accomplish? Up there in those hick towns, he deals with some nut in the synagogue, and then in this small town all the people are excited about him. Then

Peter and the others think he's going to make it big if he seizes the opportunity, and he says, "No, I think we'll just go on to some other hick towns and proclaim the good news there also. That's really what I've come to do."

It was hard for him and it was hard for the disciples and they kept getting at him about this: "This doesn't seem to be working. When are you going to establish the kingdom?" But Jesus would go to Jerusalem, the big city, only to die.

It was his way, and Jesus' way of gentleness and of sowing seeds and of mercy and nonviolence and truth burst forth into the resurrection. We have the evidence in Jesus that the little things we do are important.

But for me, it is only in faith and in hope that I trust this *is* the way, and the way that I spend my time doesn't seem so useless.

Fourth Sunday in Ordinary Time/B cycle; Mk 1:21-39.

Ken Untener

Christianity is meant to be joyful

I do lots of different kinds of work.
I am stuck with a lot of administration. I also have meetings, write letters and memos, and so forth.

In the midst of all of this, I sometimes get an opportunity to write – by that I mean to write a short article or a funny letter to some of my friends. This is different from doing "business." It is composing, writing, being creative and original.

One day, I was writing something like that and my secretary said to me, "You really enjoy that, don't you?"

I asked her what she meant and she said that something came over me when I was doing that sort of thing. It wasn't as though I started to laugh or had some kind of plastic smile. Sometimes it is even difficult – I have a deadline to meet for an article and it is frantic and hectic and sweaty.

But something comes over me and someone watching would be able to say just as she said, "You really enjoy that."

That is the kind of joy that I am talking about. It doesn't mean that everything is easy. It doesn't mean that you are smiling or laughing. There are ups and downs. There is suffering. But deep down within, there is an inner joy.

Inner joy is the trademark of Christianity.

If you don't have it, something is wrong.

It doesn't matter whether you like the priest at your parish or even the design of your parish church. You may not agree with everything . . . there may be problems.

But deep down within, is there a sense of joy?

If there isn't, then do something about it. Maybe you will need to think things through, or to pray some more, or to get some help.

But know this: Christianity is meant to be joyful. Not to be joyful is a *signal,* and you should listen to that signal.

The Lord said, "All this I tell you that my joy may be yours . . . and your joy may be complete."

Jn 15:9-11.

The priest is an orchestra leader

A few days ago, I celebrated the 19th anniversary of my ordination as a priest.

I remember the night before my ordination – that is a night for many deep reflections. In the middle of my thoughts, I remember thinking: "I wonder how a bishop feels the night before he ordains a priest?" After all, that is the moment that the bishop summons his greatest power and does what no one else could do.

Now, 19 years later, I know what a bishop thinks about the night before ordaining a priest. You know what I was thinking about last night as I was driving home down Highway 81?

I was thinking about how great it was going to be to see the people of the Church of Saginaw and the people of the wider Church at the ceremony. I was thinking of how great it was going to be to see the presbyterate gathered here, to see familiar faces from the seminary and a whole lot of other people. And I was thinking of what a great celebration it was going to be because I know that these people know how to celebrate.

Mind you, I hadn't forgotten about what's-his-name who's going to be ordained, but I was thinking about him in relationship to all these people.

Nineteen years ago, it might have been different. The focus would have been on Tom and the bishop. You would have thought about that dramatic moment when the bishop performed his task, and everyone would have watched.

That is not what I was thinking about last night. And, to me, the unconscious development of my thinking (I hadn't planned to think this way!) represents part of the great shift that has taken place in the Church during those years.

We have become much more aware of the importance of ceremony. For example, in talking about the Rite of Christian Initiation of Adults (RCIA), we realize how important it is that there be community into which the individual is received. It is no longer simply a private moment when someone is baptized. It is a public moment when someone is received into an exciting group.

The same is true of our development in understanding the sacrament of reconciliation. There has to be an identifiable group with whom the person is reconciled, if the public rite is to have its full meaning.

The same is true in our understanding of an ordination. Tom is being called forth from the group to lead the group. He is not being ordained to celebrate private Masses or to do things on his own as an individual. He is being called forth to be an orchestra leader, and the people are the orchestra.

The priesthood is many things, and it has its many joys and sorrows. But as long as you maintain the connection, the link, the living communion between you and this orchestra – the people – the priesthood need never be flat or dull or bland. It need never become drudgery. It can be hard work. It can be taxing and frustrating and all those things – but never dull and never flat and never boring.

If you stay connected with real people, it is the most adventuresome, rich kind of life that you will ever experience.

Besides, with an orchestra like that, it would be impossible to be dull.

Ordination of Tom McNamara; June 4, 1982.

'Servant of God' model

------

*T*om Gumbleton [auxiliary bishop of Detroit, Michigan], Joe Imesch [bishop of Joliet, Illinois] and I are very close friends.

Joe and I sometimes kid Tom about how different it would be for him if he had to pastor a diocese.

His life is very different from ours. He is off to El Salvador about every third week, or to some meeting of Pax Christi or Bread for the World.

When he gives talks around the Archdiocese of Detroit or around the country, these are the issues he talks about. Tom is a prophetic voice on the social-justice issues of our day, and Tom is very good at that, and Tom has the freedom to do that. I'm not referring simply to the freedom of time. It is also the freedom of being able to speak out and let the chips fall where they may.

Joe and I don't have that same freedom, and neither do many people. For us, the chips don't "fall where they may" . . . they fall in our laps.

We have a parish or a diocese to shepherd, and sometimes there are trade-offs. Sometimes you have to bite your tongue because you need to keep the family together.

Sometimes you don't fight. Sometimes you step away, as Jesus often did, and you do so not because of any lack of will to fight, but because you believe you have a God-given role to play for these people at this time in this place.

That's true of every pastor. It's true of everyone in non-specialized parish work. The Servant of God model presented in the Gospel about Jesus curing the man with the withered hand on the Sabbath speaks very much to us: "Behold my servant whom I have chosen . . . he will not contend or cry out, nor will anyone hear his voice in the streets . . . a bruised reed he will not break, a smoldering wick he will not quench . . ."

Jesus had a chance to fight, but he didn't. He withdrew. Matthew's intent in explaining this through the quote from Isaiah seems to be to show that this did not come from fear or weakness, but rather from the conviction that this was the Father's will for him. Matthew describes Jesus as fulfilling the prophecy about the Servant of God, the courageous but gentle leader often referred to as the "Suffering Servant."

There is something that rings true here about the role of a pastor and the role of others in parish ministry. I think that the Servant of God model used here of Jesus is a good description of diocesan priesthood. We have a role that is different from many others who give their lives in the service of the Church:

We are less the storm troopers . . . and more the shepherds.

We deal less with the sensational things . . . more with the ordinary joys and sorrows of life.

We are often in a situation similar to Jesus. He is not wrestling with the issue of the occupying Roman army, but with the issue of the Sabbath law and whether he could cure a crippled man. In our day-to-day ministry, we wrestle not so much with issues like the Persian Gulf, but with whether there can be a pastoral solution to a broken marriage.

We do not fill the air with prophetic shouts but with simple homilies preached on weekdays and weekends.

We are not so much in the streets as in the homes.

We deal less with great structures . . . more with the bruised reeds.

We can't pick our issues and stick with one or two. We take the ones that come, and they number in the thousands.

There's a difference between the role of a Dan Berrigan and a parish priest. There's a difference between a woman religious serving in a parish, and a Sr. Ardeth Platte protesting up at Wurtsmith Air Base in Oscoda, Michigan.

The Church needs all those roles and all those people, but there is a difference. Each of us has to ask, as apparently Jesus asked himself, "What is God calling *me* to do for *these people* at *this particular time?*"

As I look at the list of 128 diocesan priests who have gone before us, I'd have to say that I don't expect to find any of their names in the history books. I don't expect that their bones are going to be exhumed for canonization. They may name a parish hall after some of them, but not an airport.

On the other hand, there is greatness here. The Servant of God model is no mean model. There are other models, and they fit Jesus, too, because he is more than the Servant of God model. But in this passage that is what he is, and it appears to be the model that describes most of what we diocesan priests do. And there is greatness here.

It's not the kind of greatness people usually measure, but it's the kind that is measured in the kingdom.

Mass for deceased priests; Mt 12:14-21; November 8, 1990.

Finding God in the poor - or not

Matthew's Gospel is characterized by the great sermons of Jesus. Jesus' last sermon before his death and resurrection contains the passage where Jesus talks about the Last Judgment, the sheep, and the goats . . . "I was hungry . . . I was thirsty . . ."

One of the things that makes this passage even more powerful is the fact that this is not a parable. Jesus will use some allegorical details such as sheep and goats and right and left and fire, but he is not saying (as he sometimes says), "The kingdom of God is something like a tree . . ." or something like that.

He is telling us what the Lord God *will* be asking when we come before him at death. He tells us what the heart of his teaching is and what the measure of our holiness shall be, and that casts it in a different light.

I've been a priest for 24 years. I've listened to people tell their sins many, many times. I would say that, in listening to those sins (and in listening to my own), I don't find that we place the times that we did not respond to those in need as the great sins. I don't find that these come off as the heart and the center of sin.

Somehow, along the way, we have displaced these from the centerpiece, and have seemed to place others (which are sins) at the center. But, as Jesus tells the story, what the Lord God shall ask us as the most important expression of sin are these.

On the other side, I must remember that the ways we care for those in need are the greatest virtues. Come the judgment, the greatest things that we have done will be to have extended a consoling touch, a word, a smile to those who in so many different ways are hungry, thirsty, strangers, in prison.

One of the best people I ever knew in reaching out to the poor was old Msgr. Clem Kern in Detroit, now dead. He was legendary for his way of going out to all people, rich and poor, but especially the poor.

I'll never forget one day talking to him in his old age about the life of a priest, and talking about where you find God in your day-to-day life. And he said something that knocked me off my chair.

He said, "Well, I'll tell you one thing, Ken. It's awfully hard to find God in the poor."

I thought, "I had always believed that is why he did this – because it was so easy to find God there."

I've never forgotten his words because I think they're so true.

It's not as though we reach out to those who are poor in so many different ways because it's a wonderful feeling and God is manifest. Only with a very deep faith can we believe the words of the Gospel that say that the Lord is there and that's reality.

And that is where our faith is real or not real.

Christ the King/A cycle; Mt 25:31-46; Holy Trinity Parish in Bay City; November 22, 1987.

A good life

On a trip to visit my mother, I was riding with my sister who, for many years, has done temporary work with different firms – law firms, corporations.

She's good at word processing and things like that.

She said, "Wherever I go, after I'm there a couple of weeks, I ask people over lunch if they like what they're doing. You know, most people don't seem to."

Then she said, "I'm surprised most people aren't excited about what they are doing, but you seem to like what you're doing. How come?"

Then I said something quite dumb. "Well, it puts you in the thick of life" (so far so good) "and it beats manufacturing bottle caps." Dumb.

And the reason it was dumb was because priesthood is good – but not because something else isn't.

I just want to say that up front because, I guess, we tend to do that. If priesthood is a good life, it doesn't mean lay ministry is not a good life, too. If you think that women ought to be ordained, it doesn't mean that men shouldn't. One isn't good because the other isn't.

And my sister was right.

I do like what I'm doing.

Fifth Sunday of Easter/C cycle; Jn 13:31-33, 34-35; ordination of Michael Dunckel; May 17, 1992.

Part V
*God has connected me with people
who were good for me . . .*

God has connected me with people who were good for me . . .

—ɯɯ—

When Ken was in eighth or ninth grade, his older sister gave him a gift of several months of music lessons from a fellow who played in cocktail lounges. The man taught him how to create his own arrangements and how to play by ear. Ken later said he learned more from that piano player than from his lessons as a child, and he often used music as an analogy in his talks.

A key question for him was: "How do I find the music in people?" A skilled leader, he believed, finds out how to get the music *out* of people.

Speaking engagements carried Ken around the world and introduced him to folks from all walks of life. Wherever he went, he made it a point to talk to people. He was curious about what they did for a living, what they thought of the Church, etc. Airline pilots explained aviation to him. Monks showed him how to grow grapes for wine. Parents told him about the perils and joys of raising children. People told him what they liked and didn't like about the Mass and the homilies.

Taking to heart the teachings of the Second Vatican Council, Ken worked to provide opportunities for all people to participate in the Church. As bishop of Saginaw, he commissioned hundreds of lay ministers, giving laity a larger role in parish life. Because the diocese had no Catholic college or university, he opened a Saginaw campus of Assumption University from Windsor, Ontario. He supported and expanded women's roles in the Church. He pushed for inclusive language in diocesan documents, prayers, and talks, and recognized the gifts and concerns of Hispanic, Native-American, and African-American Catholics. Ken set up a Community Affairs Committee, drawing together civic and Church leaders for a monthly Friday breakfast to discuss local issues. He helped bring a Boys and Girls Club to Saginaw.

And he focused on the poor.

At the annual diocesan Chrism Mass in 1991, he challenged people to begin each parish meeting for the next six months with the question, "How will what we are doing here affect the poor?" The decree brought him nationwide attention.

"Jesus wasn't telling us to become poor. He was warning us about how we who are not poor can construct a life that cuts us off from the poor. We can insulate ourselves from two-thirds of the world," he said.

At an *ad limina* meeting at the Vatican, Pope John Paul II told Ken that his Saginaw diocese needed discipline. "No, your holiness," Ken replied. "My diocese needs compassion." To Ken Untener, no one was insignificant.

At the 125th anniversary of St. Mary's Cathedral in Saginaw in 1991, he reminded people at Mass, "When we die, just about the only thing that will matter is the way we treated people. I say that after much thought and I don't use those words carelessly . . . The measure of our greatness, or our holiness, is the way we treat insignificant people."

People who shaped my life

————————

We all saw in the press the dramatic moment when Pope John Paul II forgave the guy who tried to kill him. Pictures of the event were all over. It *was* a wonderful thing – a great symbolic action.

I was reading the letters to the editor in Time magazine a little while afterward (I do a lot of heavy reading), and one of the letters to the editor said, "The pope's *supposed* to forgive people, so what's the big deal?"

There was probably a touch of cynicism in that, but I think a touch of truth, too. I would have to say that if somebody I knew really well – a regular person – forgave somebody who did him in – that would have more effect on me.

That's what shapes my life. That's what has shaped my life. It's the people who don't do forgiveness "professionally," but who just do it because they believe it makes sense.

People have been salt to my life that way – around the kitchen table, or over a beer, or anywhere. People who were willing to disagree and make me think. People who were willing to say that they were wrong and that they fell on their face. That sure helped me. People who were truthful, people who were refreshing. That's what shaped my life. Normal people.

I was in Albuquerque, New Mexico, a couple of years ago, and I borrowed a car (it was an old car) to go from where I was to visit somebody in another town. While I was driving, the car overheated. One of the hoses blew, actually. I was on a back road and didn't have any tools.

After a while, this fellow came along who must have been in his mid-20s. He stopped and saw the problem and helped me out. He had some tools, and we worked on it together for about 25 minutes, and managed to put the car back so it would run again.

When he finished, I said, "Gee, I'm really grateful. Thank you."

He said, "Well, now, you see what I have done. I have given the power of Jesus' love to you. I have given you the love Jesus has given to all of us. Now that you have received the power of Jesus, you go and give that power of love to somebody else."

Well, he got in his car and drove off.

The stuff that moves me is the people – the salt of the earth, the people who live their life because they think it makes sense. Who forgive and who love, who dream, pray, who search.

That's the salt of the earth.

Fifth Sunday/A cycle; Mt 13-16.

An old Chicago priest

---

*I*t was about 15 years ago, and I was giving a retreat for some Chicago priests. One of them, old Andy McDonough, a tall, tough-looking but kindly-looking priest, told a story.

He and a couple of his cronies were on their day off, and were at a rectory playing cards in the evening. A young priest happened by, and he asked these veteran priests, "If you had it to do over again, and you knew what you know now, would you become a priest?"

Andy said that he thought about it for a moment and then said to him, "Yes. Yes, I would. You probably expected that answer. But the big thing is *why* I would.

"It's not so much that the bishops I've had were all that supportive of me, although I can't complain. And it's not so much that the people were always so good to me, although I'd have to say that they were. But that's not the reason.

"Nor is it because I did everything so well. I did my best, but I made some mistakes.

"Because it's an easy life? No. It's a good life, but not always easy.

"Here's the reason. It's because, as I look back, God worked through me. God was able to use me to do some good. There were times when my homily wasn't so good, but I believed what I said and God let my faith show through to some people, and it helped them. There were times when my words of advice were fumbling but, by God, they helped some people.

"As I look back, I can see the hand of God in my life. God managed to use me to do some good. *That's* why I'd do it over."

We can ask that kind of question of ourselves. If you had to do it over again, would you take up the kind of profession, the kind of work you've done most of your life? Would you have stayed in this part of the world? Would you marry the person you married? Why? Or why not?

Here's a question we might not think of asking: If you had to do it over again, would you be a Christian? Would you let yourself be baptized? Which is to say, would you be a disciple of Jesus?

If the answer is yes, the next question is: *Why?*

Some might say, "I didn't have a choice. My parents decided that for me." Well, at some point, you still had a choice. A lot of people were baptized as infants and never followed through.

Some might say, "The only other option was to die and go to hell!" But that's not really true. Church teaching is very clear and explicit: Non-Christians can get to heaven.

Maybe it would help if we tried to think about why Peter, Andrew, James, and John became disciples. They made this choice as adults, and they weren't out looking for something to do. They were businessmen. To become disciples of Jesus, they had to leave some things behind. What would they say if we asked them years later whether they'd do it again? I can picture them saying something like this:

"We had heard Jesus speak a few times. He'd been up our way in Galilee awhile. He was, as they say, 'proclaiming the good news of God.' And it *was* good news. Jesus was talking about a 'God-project' that was called 'the kingdom of God.' It was a new way of seeing things – an earth with a future, a human race with a future. We wanted to be part of this . . . part of making the earth and all creation what it is meant to be – not a place of tyrants, war, starvation, people living in hovels. Something new was underway, and Jesus was heading it up. He said that his work involved people, and Jesus wanted us to be part of it. And we *wanted* to be part of it. We were drawn to Jesus and what he was doing. That's why we did it, and that's why we'd do it again."

What do you think Mary would have said if asked toward the end of her life, "Would you say 'yes' if, when you were visited by the angel Gabriel, you knew what you know now?" Mary would say, "Of course. You can talk if you like about my 'seven sorrows,' but look at what I was part of! I wouldn't miss that for the world."

But we don't have to go back 2,000 years. What do you think Mother Teresa would have said toward the end of her time? She'd do it over. And why? Because she was forced? Because she didn't want to go to hell? No. Because this "God-project" – helping to build the reign of God – struck a beautiful chord in her heart, and she wanted to be part of it.

It would be interesting, wouldn't it, to be in a small group of people whom we trust and talk about whether we'd do it over – be baptized, be disciples of the Lord – and why we would or wouldn't do it. It would be interesting, even without a group, to talk it over with the Lord. Maybe I can do that sometime today or sometime this week.

I wonder what I'd say – not the "yes" or the "no."

The interesting part would be the "why."

Third Sunday in Ordinary Time/B cycle; Mk 1:14-20; January 26, 2003.

Cardinal Edward Mooney

I would like to tell a personal story, a true story that crystallizes for me the meaning of the Gospel of the rich man who didn't know what to do with his harvest.

It is a story about Cardinal Edward Mooney of Detroit.

I never knew him personally, but our lives intersected by strange coincidence.

On August 3, 1937, Cardinal Mooney was installed as Archbishop of Detroit.

That is the day I was born. I was the seventh of nine children, and by that time my mother was running out of names. So she chose as my middle name, Edward, since I was born the day Edward Cardinal Mooney was appointed to Detroit.

That was the first intersection of our lives.

Seventeen years later, when I finished high school, I wanted to enter the seminary. However, there was a problem with my leg (largely corrected since then) and Church law prohibited people with such physical problems from becoming priests. The rector of the seminary went to see Cardinal Mooney about it, and he decided that he could bend the law enough to accept me. If it were not for him, I might never have been able to become a priest.

That was the second intersection of our lives.

Three years later, when I was in college seminary, Pope Pius XII died. The cardinals gathered in Rome to elect a new pope, and Cardinal Mooney became the first Detroit archbishop to participate in a papal election.

The day the cardinals were to enter the conclave that would elect Pope John XXIII, Cardinal Mooney died. They brought his body back to Detroit for a great funeral to be held at the cathedral. I sang in the choir at his funeral. He was to be buried in a crypt at St. John's Seminary.

Cardinal Mooney had built St. John's Seminary. In many ways, it was his life's dream. Once it was built, he spent his summers there. St. John's has a nine-hole golf course because Cardinal Mooney liked golf.

He also built his own grave. Below the main chapel, there were a number of crypt chapels where faculty members could say daily Mass, and in the floor right in front of one of those crypt altars, Cardinal Mooney had a grave built.

It was all prepared. Even the brass letters and numerals for the cover of the crypt were prepared. Of course, he didn't know the day he was going to die, so he purchased a whole set of numbers so that they could just choose the right ones for his death.

Well, this is where the funeral procession went after the Mass at the cathedral – out to the seminary at Plymouth.

Cardinal Mooney's funeral was the biggest funeral Detroit had ever had up until then, and the biggest since then. Detroit has never had a larger funeral. I rode in the funeral procession from the cathedral to Plymouth, and I shall never forget it. People lined the streets from the cathedral to Plymouth. Thirty miles . . . and you drove through a continuous line of people.

What a sight it was! Cardinal Mooney, you see, was a very famous person. Before coming to Detroit, he had been Vatican envoy to India. Then when he came to Detroit, he became the first Detroit archbishop ever to be named a cardinal. There were fewer cardinals back then and, in a way, it was even more prestigious than it is now.

Furthermore, Cardinal Mooney had the charisma of an Irish politician, and he was frequently in the papers. He was well-known and much loved by people throughout the country, to say nothing of the people in Detroit. So, they turned out by the thousands for his funeral cortege.

As we were driving through that wall of people, I remember saying to the priest who was driving the car that this might present some problems for the seminary. After all, people would be coming out there all the time visiting his grave.

The priest turned to me and said, "Ken, there is nobody deader than a dead bishop."

Nineteen years later, quite by surprise to me and to everyone else, I was sent to St. John's Seminary to be rector there. That is the last intersection of our lives.

I never, never saw anyone visit Cardinal Mooney's crypt. The crypt chapels are still there, and they are not in an out-of-the-way place. St. John's Seminary is much more accessible now with expressways.

I never, never saw anyone visit that grave.

I do not say that in criticism as though people should be streaming out there. When you're dead, you're dead. That's the way it is.

Perhaps I'm the only visitor. I cut through that way frequently because it is a short cut between my room and my office at the other end of the building. Sometimes I stop and spend a few moments in quiet reflection before that grave.

I look down and I see my birth date – the day he was appointed to Detroit – and his death date. And as I stand there in the darkness and the stillness and the loneliness of the place, my mind flashes back to that solid wall of people from Detroit to Plymouth on the day he was buried. It's gone, all gone.

That is the daily meditation that keeps this Gospel in my life. Our Lord wasn't saying that material things and concerns are unimportant. They are important. Your job, the acquisition of material goods, the problems and concerns of this world . . . these are important.

But they're relative. They're not all *that* important. They pass away, and there are other things far more important in life that last forever.

I think about Cardinal Mooney, his fame, those crowds, the important decisions he made, the financial worries of the Archdiocese of Detroit, and those red robes . . . and I think, "All those things were important, but do you know what was really important in Cardinal Mooney's life . . . the things that offered the possibility of richness and wealth in heaven, the things that the people up there remember and cherish? Do you know what it was?

"The way he treated the guy at the gas station, or the time he was patient with somebody who was boring, the times he spoke sincerely and truthfully and simply, with no motivation but love."

That is the way it is for you and me.

We all have responsibilities and they are important. But they could not compare in importance with those things that make you rich in the sight of God – some extra time spent with your children, or a word of forgiveness for someone with whom you have been on the outs, or some moments in your life to think a little bit and to pray, or a smile in the supermarket to someone who looks sour.

Those are the things that are important, and they are far more important than the money, the car, the job, the recognition. The things that will all pass away.

Eighteenth Sunday in Ordinary Time/C cycle; Lk 12:13-21.

In the face of death

On Sunday, I was asked to stop at a home and visit someone who was dying of cancer. She is in her late 50s or early 60s, probably has a couple of weeks left, but perfectly clear thinking.

I was talking to her, and I asked her if she was okay with facing her death. I wanted to help her, if I could.

She said to me (it knocked me over), "I'm not afraid to die because 25 years ago, I had a heart problem and I died."

Well, now she didn't really die – she wasn't brain dead – but the heart stopped and the doctors thought they lost her, and they *did* lose her for awhile.

She said, "I remember, I shall never forget, the peace. I was going to God and I heard this music. I can't tell you how beautiful it was.

"I remember my kids were little then. I remember somehow having to choose whether to come back and raise my children, or go to this wonderful, peaceful, beautiful place to which I was going.

"I remember deciding that I better help those kids."

She said, "I'm not afraid to die. I've been through the beginning of it, and it is one of the most beautiful experiences of my whole life, and I can't put it into words."

I'll tell you something. Sitting there, listening to that woman, gave me great, good feelings about death, and about faith, and the life that awaits us.

Eighth grade prayer service at the Cathedral of Mary of the Assumption in Saginaw; May 11, 1995.

D-Day

---

*J*esus *raised his eyes to heaven and prayed.*
It's touching to hear Jesus pray for us that way.

He's like a grandmother or a grandfather who wants us to be together, to get along.

I'm touched sometimes when I hear children tell me that they pray that their parents will stop fighting. I hear parents pray that their children will stop fighting. Pastors pray that their parish won't fight. Bishops pray that the parishes won't fight.

None of us wants people to fight, to not to get along. We all want people to be one. We really do, but it's hard. It's hard for us (even with people we're close to) not to be mean to one another, but to be kind, patient.

A couple of years ago, it was a Sunday and I was celebrating Mass at the cathedral. It was the 50th anniversary of D-Day in the Second World War, when the United States Army and some other countries were trying to fight their way into Europe, and the German armies were resisting.

Now to feel what happened, you have to understand the way they had the chairs set up at the cathedral at that time. They had a whole lot of them all facing this way, and then they had a whole lot of them on this side facing that way, and the altar was in the middle.

I was out there talking and I said, "Is there anybody here who lost a family member on D-Day?"

This old woman raised her hand over here.

I said, "Whom did you lose?"

She said, "My brother."

And I said, "Where did it happen, and who was he with – the Navy, Army . . . ?"

She explained.

Then I said, "Is there anybody else?"

There was an old woman over here.

I said, "And whom did you lose?"

And she said, "My brother."

And I said, "And where did that happen?"

She paused a second – and I shall never, ever until I die, forget this – she said, "He was in the German army."

Their brothers had been shooting at each other. Each man was trying to do his duty. But to see their sisters sitting there, looking at each other, with the altar table there where we were gathered together, I couldn't speak for some seconds.

In that moment, I realized why Jesus prayed so hard the night before he died, "That they would all be one," and that the fighting would stop.

School Mass at St. Stephen Grade School, Saginaw; Jn 17:20-26; May 23, 1996.

'Stutz'

---

*F*r. Gerry "Stutz" Brennan and I had something of a father-son relationship.

Our paths first crossed the summer before I entered the seminary. I was 17 and worked at Camp Sancta Maria (a summer camp for boys in northern Michigan). By then he was on the faculty at Sacred Heart Seminary in Detroit, and had already begun to build St. Joseph Parish in Dearborn, Michigan.

That summer he handed me a hammer to help him build a cabin at Camp Sancta Maria.

A couple of years later, in the seminary, he handed me (figuratively) a baton to help him direct his seminary choir.

When I was ordained a priest, he handed me a vestment, one I still wear a lot now.

When I became a bishop, he handed me a crosier, one he'd had made that telescoped all together.

He handed me a lot of things in between and ever since, and he did the same for many other people.

He handed me an appointment book every year, and taught me to use the micro-elite type on a typewriter in order to jam the back of the book with information and names and addresses and everything under the sun.

He handed me my first full set of golf clubs.

He handed me a lot of friends that I otherwise would not have known, because Stutz never kept his friends to himself. That included a lot of priest friends because Stutz's door was always open to characters of all kinds and all ages, to gather around the supper table or the bridge table, or just sit around and talk.

It was Stutz who taught me preaching in the seminary.

It was Stutz who taught me to give things away, not carefully metered out, but almost recklessly, as Jesus gave away his mercy. When Stutz lost money at bridge or gin rummy or golf, he always gave an equal amount to charity because (as he told me once), "If I can afford to lose it in a bet, I can afford to give it to a good cause."

So when he lost, he always lost double.

But what Stutz gave me most of all was a hard-rock faith.

I always thought Stutz and St. Peter were probably a lot alike.

It was Peter who never seemed to lack for self-confidence. When Jesus walked on water, Peter said, "Show me how and I can do that too."

It was Peter who didn't like to spend a lot of time thinking about things, but moved swiftly to action, as when he jumped in the water and swam to shore and left the others to row the boat. One of Stutz's sayings to me that I repeat very often is, "Ken, sometimes the best way to do something is to do it."

It was Peter who always seemed to ask the practical question. When the Lord was talking about forgiveness, Peter spoke up and said, "How about putting a number on that. Maybe 7?"

Fr. Brennan's eye for the bottom line on the account sheet was never because he cared that much about money in itself. He didn't at all. For him, money was a measure of reality. It was an indicator of whether or not we were connecting with real life. The money question always forced you to be down-to-earth. Sometimes he thought that bishops weren't as practical as they ought to be, and when I became bishop, he suggested that I take as my motto: "A buck's a buck." Stutz was many things, but he was not a poet.

Many a Saturday morning or Sunday morning, I sat at the breakfast table with Fr. Brennan and Ed Lundy [a parishioner and the treasurer of the Ford Motor Company], and it was like attending the graduate school of real life. What a combination. There was Ed with his brilliance in economics and just about everything else I can think of, and Stutz punctuating the conversation with occasional comments such as, "That's true but fairly pedestrian," or "That's a possibility," or "That's basically stupid." I learned a lot, and those are among my happiest memories.

Many an evening I sat in the living room at St. Joseph's with Stutz, the air filled with his cigarette smoke and my cigar smoke (really it was *his* cigar smoke because he gave me the cigar in the first place) and we talked of many things.

Often we talked about the Lord. In those conversations, the Lord was never an abstraction. It was never a "puffy" Jesus that we talked about. It was the carpenter from Nazareth who understood lumber . . . and tools . . . and money . . . and people.

Fr. Brennan's faith was a very practical, hard-rock, real, honest faith. If the Lord had ever asked him, "Do you love me more than these?" I can picture him saying pretty much what St. Peter said. I can picture him saying, "Well, let's begin with the bottom line. Lord, you know that I love you." And he did.

Fr. Brennan did not lack for self-confidence in most everything, but in relationship to the Lord, he was a humble man. Fr. Brennan never thought that he was particularly holy. He did not even think that he was quite ready to die. But this he knew, "Yes, Lord, I love you." And he did.

I remember when Cardinal Edward Mooney [cardinal of the Detroit Archdiocese] was buried back in 1958. I was a young seminarian and I rode with Fr. Brennan in the funeral procession out to the grave at St. John's Seminary.

All the way from the cathedral to Plymouth, the streets were lined with people. It was the biggest funeral Detroit ever had, before or since. I said to Fr. Brennan, "This is probably going to create a lot of problems for St. John's Seminary in the future because of all the people that will be going out to visit the grave."

And he said to me, "Ken, basically, there's nothing deader than a dead priest."

Well, maybe so, but I think not with Fr. Brennan.

There are too many quotable quotes to remember.

There are too many incidents to retell.

There are too many buildings he built that are still standing.

Too many clothes that he gave away that are still being worn.

Too many lives he touched.

Funeral Mass for Fr. Gerard S. Brennan; August 24, 1992.

Sr. Anna Mae

Sr. Anna Mae had five Unteners in the first grade at St. Charles Grade School (not all at once – we were spread out a bit.)

My sister, Mary Ann, was the first, and I was the fifth. Before I even started school, the name "Sr. Anna Mae" was a household world.

It occurred to me that I have come back here [to the motherhouse in Monroe, Michigan] for the funeral of two of the sisters who were part of my life at St. Charles. A few years back, it was Sr. Marie Isabel, who was principal when I was in the 12th grade.

Now it's Sr. Anna Mae who taught me in the first grade. So, my early formation – first grade through 12th grade – is more or less "framed" by IHM [Sisters, Servants of the Immaculate Heart of Mary] sisters, and that is something for which I am very grateful.

My first grade memories are very clear. It was a long time ago, but it is still very, very present to me. I remember this short, "roundish" person, dressed in blue, with a look on her face that was just plain good. I couldn't describe it, but clearly it was a look of peace and joy.

Well, those are memories. I've got some data to back them up.

You know the short autobiography that each sister is to write about herself? I've got the one Sr. Anna Mae wrote a few years ago. Listen to how she begins:

"I was born on January 9, 1914, to Gertrude and William Nadeau and two years later my brother joined our family. I grew up surrounded by love and joy."

I was telling Mary Ann that when I read this autobiography yesterday, I was struck by how often Anna Mae talks about "joy." Anna Mae didn't realize it when she was writing this, but you can't miss it when you read it. Everything was a joy to her, and it's right here at the beginning of her autobiography.

When she was 19 years old, she was assigned to St. Charles, and she writes: *My life there was filled with **joy** . . . except for the year* *that Mary Ann was in my class."* What she *really* wrote was, *"My life there was filled with **joy** and love and lasted for 11 years."*

Toward the middle of her life, when she was appointed Primary Supervisor of the IHM schools, she wrote: *"It was a **joy** to help beginning teachers and working with them to make them better and professional teachers."*

Finally, when she was 72 years old, toward the final years of her life, she came back home to Monroe, and she talked about going to St. Patrick Parish in Carleton two days a week to help children in reading and math. She writes: *"My **joy** for the other three days was to work on the third floor of the [motherhouse] infirmary. What a grace to serve these beautiful sisters who can no longer care for themselves."*

When you read this, you find joy at the beginning, joy in the middle, joy along the way, and joy at the end. It's remarkable.

I also noticed in the other written pieces about Anna Mae – "The Remembrance" – something that is very interesting. It says: *"Anna Mae had the practice in her elder years of writing one joy in her notebook each day."*

As I think about it, I could do that. It's not a huge enterprise. It would take about 15 seconds. Imagine what would happen if I did that, even on a bad day. To celebrate how God shone through the stained glass of my life.

One joy – can you imagine what would happen if the whole world did that? What a different spirit would be in the air.

I'm going to start doing that. I never thought of it before. And when I do it tonight – for the first time – the joy will be that I was here, with the people who loved Anna Mae, and part of a liturgy that celebrated how God shone through the stained-glass window of her life.

If I do that, not just tonight but every day . . . maybe, maybe I'll develop the indescribably kind and peaceful smile of Sr. Anna Mae.

I'll ask her to help me.

Funeral Mass for Sr. Anna Mae Nadeau, IHM; Sisters, Servants of the Immaculate Heart of Mary Motherhouse in Monroe, Michigan; Jn 15:9-12; August 7, 2002.

Angel of God's presence

W as Jack Gentner afraid to die?
Well, yes and no.

Some months ago, when it became clear that medical procedures couldn't save him from certain death, I had a long talk with Jack. I asked him, "What's it like to look death in the eye?"

He said, "I'm having a hard time. Pray for me."

And pray I did because I knew what he meant.

Four weeks ago this very day, when we buried Fr. Charlie O'Neil, I went early in the morning to visit Jack. We had another long talk. I asked how he was doing in the face of death.

He said, "I'm doing better. Keep praying."

A week ago today when I was homeward bound, I talked to Jack on the car phone from somewhere in Wyoming. I asked him again, and he said, "I'm okay."

There's no question that what helped Jack through this was the remarkable presence and love and faith and care of his family, close friends, priests' support group, parish staff, parishioners, former parishioners, and everyone who did a kind thing for him, or said a good word to him, or prayed a good prayer for him.

This was the "angel of God's presence" for Jack.

Was Jack Gentner afraid to die? Yes and no, but in the end, it was a death he freely accepted.

What would help me in the face of certain death?

I'll tell you one thing that would help: To be part of a believing community.

The disciples weren't a lot of help to Jesus, but the community of disciples was a great help to Jack and would mean the world to me.

When I look around and see people in graced moments, see the faith in their eyes, hear them sing and say their faith aloud, and realize that they, too, hold these down deep, hard-to-believe truths, I am struck with faith, hope, and love.

What would help me in the face of certain death? The Word of God.

The Bible we placed on Jack's casket was his own Bible. The family used it in praying with him, especially in those last days, and I was with them for some of that on Saturday evening. Jack had marked and underlined many passages and written notes in the margin. I wondered to myself, "What passages would I want to hear in those last hours?" I hope everyone has a marked-up Bible that is a personal treasury of prayer.

What would help me in the face of certain death?

More than anything else, I think it would be the experience embedded in my heart of having participated in the Eucharist over and over and over. Faced with death, I'd want to be able to say, "This is not entirely new territory for me. I have joined with the Lord Jesus at Eucharist in his dying and rising. I have traversed this road and rehearsed this moment a thousand times."

Times like this make me resolve that I will not glide so easily over the familiar words of the eucharistic prayers.

What will help us in the face of certain death?

The Lord himself will help us.

It's interesting that for his funeral Mass, Jack chose a first reading with the words: ". . . who will rescue me from this doomed body? Thanks be to God – it is done through Jesus Christ our Lord."

Funeral Mass for Fr. Jack Gentner; Lk 22:39-46; May 7, 1997.

Drawn to our destiny

I was recently on a flight across the country. A pilot sat next to me, going to pick up his next flight.

He flew one of the large 767s.

I got talking to him, and I asked him about instrument landings because I don't like instrument landings.

He said, "Oh, the new planes have the capability of landing in what they call 'zero-zero'." That means that while you're in the air, you can see zero feet in front of you, and also when you land, you can see zero feet in front of you. Pea soup.

He told me he had done it twice.

I remarked that to land in total blindness like that, you'd really have to trust your instruments.

He explained that they have three computers on board, each of which is checking to make sure everything is correct. If just one of those computers disagrees with the other two, they abort the landing, circle, and do it again. All three computers, checking the same data, have to agree that everything is correct in order to bring the plane safely home.

We can easily picture our life as a flight whose landing will take us through the darkness of death safely home, we hope, to God.

How do we know that our heart is headed in the right direction?

What is drawing our heart to its destiny? We need to double-check, triple-check the flight path bringing us home.

I'll tell you one of the ways we do that.

At the Eucharist, we take some of our money and give it to the Lord. This is the real stuff of life. It comes from our job, our budget, our wallet, our life. It's our treasure and it is brought right up here to the altar. We put it in God's hands and, in doing so, we put our hearts there. Bread and wine are also brought forward – food, which is also our treasure. We put everything in the hands of the Lord.

In doing so, we join with Jesus who, when he died, entrusted everything, his entire life, to the Father. At every Eucharist we set ourselves on a true course, for we follow the Lord who is the Way, the Truth, and the Life.

St. Augustine had it right: Our hearts were made for you, O God, and they will not rest until they rest in you.

The Lord tells us how to do that: "Where your treasure is, there also will your heart be."

Cathedral of Mary of the Assumption in Saginaw; Lk 12:32-48; August 8-9, 1998.

Doc Fulgenzi

$\mathcal{A}$ week ago, I buried a doctor.

His name was Doc Fulgenzi, and he was 94 years old.

He was from the east side of Detroit (same side of the city that I came from) and had been dying for three or four years from lung cancer. But he was as alert and sharp all the way to the end as a person could be.

He spent his last days up in Saginaw, and I got to know him very well because he liked golf and I like golf. He couldn't play anymore, but after a Sunday morning of Masses and before a Sunday evening of whatever, I'd often sit down and watch a golf tournament with him.

He was finally taken to St. Mary's Hospital, and it was (we were pretty sure) the end. He was still as bright and alert as could be, but his lungs had begun to clog, possibly because of pneumonia or congestion.

I had to leave for San Jose, California, for a weeklong retreat that I was to give for the priests out there. On the way to the airport, I stopped to see Doc. I figured that this was going to be the last time I'd see him alive on this earth, and I didn't know whether I should say the prayers of anointing or the prayers for the dying. I had with me the book that a priest carries in his pocket, and there's only one page between those two prayers. It's a whole set of prayers for the sick and the anointing of the sick, and you turn the page and it's the prayer for the dying.

I didn't know what I was going to say.

Doc didn't talk about dying right then. He knew he was dying, but he had grit and perhaps thought that he would get through this episode. I wasn't sure, and what do you say? So we spent some time together and we talked. I never did pull the prayers for the dying. It just didn't seem the right thing to do.

But as I was leaving the room (and again, I figured this was the last time I would see him), he pointed to me and he said very emphatically, "I'm praying for you."

And I said, "I'm praying for you."

Those were pretty good last words, and they were the last words.

I don't feel bad that I didn't say the prayers for the dying, because you just go with what is the right thing to say. But I've never regretted that my last words were, "I'm praying for you."

Doc knew what he was saying, and I knew what he was saying.

And that's plenty.

Physicians' Evening Prayer; October 25, 2001.

The Amish

*T*he other day I went out to make some communion calls. You go a long way to make communion calls because there aren't that many parishes in the County of Clare in Michigan (there's only two).

It was a snowy morning. I was on the back roads, and along down the road I see a horse and buggy coming toward me.

I drove by it and I'll be darned if I don't go another mile or two, and there's another horse and buggy coming toward me. The snow was falling gently. It was quiet and it just seemed so interesting and nice. I began noticing that there were Amish people in that area, and I was looking at the different farms as I drove by.

How can you tell an Amish farm? There's no tractor. But what if it was cold and all the tractors were in the barn (or wherever they keep the tractors)? How would you still know that it's an Amish farm? No electrical poles running to the house. Of course, there are other ways. A lot of men have beards (but not everyone who has a beard is Amish), and the Amish wear clothes that are a lot different.

Well, it was interesting because in that little trip, I came across a lot of Amish people. One guy was on a wagon and he had his little son (about two or three years old) in it, standing there as he was driving the horses. I was thinking: They are so different!

And, on that snowy, quiet day the difference was kind of nice.

Then I began to think: You know, we're *all* different! All of us Christians are different. Oh, we believe in electricity and we use tractors and cars and telephones. That's not why we're different. But we're different for a lot of other reasons, and the differences ought to show up more.

Just like you can point to somebody and say: "Look at them. I know they're Amish because there is a horse and a buggy and there are no electrical poles and there's no tractor," folks ought to be able to point to us and say: "Oh yes, that's one of those Christians. Did you ever notice how they treat people? They're so kind to everyone, even in the stores. As a matter of fact, I hear they have this thing: They love their enemies. Really different. And they do some things that are so charming and so wonderful. Like, they give things away. They're always looking for people who need things, and they're always giving things away – seems like all the time.

"And they can tell you stories. They can tell the most fascinating stories of this man, Jesus. And they dream great dreams – they talk about a kingdom and a banquet, and they talk about everybody being part of the royal family.

"And they see things so differently. They love this earth. They say it's God's world – God's got the world in his hands. They reverence trees and little animals and their streams and their crops. It's like they talk about this world: God is in it.

"Christians just see things differently from anybody else. Oh, they are strange people, these Christians. They are strange and wonderful. They believe in life after death, and they pray to people who have died and with people who have died. It's wonderful."

I got to thinking about that as I drove home that day. We're that different, and that difference has to show up.

Family Mass, St. Philip Neri Parish in Coleman; February 10, 1988.

Power of silence

I met with a Maryknoll missionary who was returning to Japan. He said that his particular apostolate in Japan was to be in dialogue with the Buddhists.

I asked him how he does this since there is so little in common.

He said that they talk things over, but the most productive engagement is when they pray together . . . in silence. After doing that for a while, he said, you experience a closeness that you didn't have before.

At about the same time, I talked to someone who had just returned from a 30-day silent retreat – the "exercises" of St. Ignatius.

There were 30-some people making this retreat, and each of them did an hour of silent prayer in the chapel four times each day. Some of them happened to choose pretty much the same times and, thus, were together in silence frequently.

At the end of the retreat, they got together like old friends and even wanted to have a reunion next year.

The interior life can do that. I think the separated churches of Christianity need to do more of that. We have to come to pray together, to be together at the interior level.

1999 Diocesan Ecumenical Service; Jn 14:21-28.

Rose Watson

$\mathcal{R}$ose Watson taught us how to handle well the difficulty of being rich.

It seems a strange thing to say: *the difficulty of being rich.*

It sounded strange when Jesus said it, too.

In comparison to most people in the world, I am rich. But Rose Watson was a few steps beyond most of us in that category, and thus her example in dealing with this difficulty is a more powerful one, a picture painted in broader strokes, a brighter light from which we can learn a greater lesson.

What is it that makes it hard for the rich to enter the kingdom of heaven?

Well, for one thing, it is hard for the rich to get *interested* in the kingdom of God. The more you have, the more you are able to build your own kingdom, your own "controlled environment." Everything is nicely provided for – food, clothes, a house (or houses), transportation, people to care for you, social status, security. It's something like youngsters with plenty of pop in the refrigerator and potato chips in the cupboard and a DVD. They don't want to go into the fresh air outside.

It's hard for the rich person to get interested in the fresh air of the kingdom.

Rose Watson handled that difficulty well. She never pretended to build a secure and enclosed world unto herself. She went into the fresh air outside – her parish, her neighborhood, her city. She took her place in a community much larger than her own private world, and her place didn't always have to be at the head of the table. She welcomed strangers, not simply in passing, but she connected her life with theirs.

I learned a lot about Rose Watson by reading letters written by people she had helped. They were put together in albums for the 25th anniversary of the Rose Watson Foundation.

There is a refrain that runs through them, a refrain best captured in one brief excerpt: *"When I first arrived at the Watson Scholarship dinner*

. . . I was overcome a bit by the friendliness and acceptance of the other recipients. Most of all, I think I was floored by the fact that as soon as I mentioned my name to you, you seemed to know all about me already. And I felt up to then that I was a real nobody. The experience of those dinners and the many other people and experiences that the scholarship grant made possible to me, helped me get over my fear of people . . ."

Imagine that – Rose Watson making a 17-year-old boy feel important. He never forgot it.

Rose Watson had a thoughtful, genuine and abiding interest in people who were outside her own private world. Here is an excerpt from another letter: *"It is difficult to express how much your support during my four years at college meant. Your postcards and Christmas cards during those years showed me your interest, and enabled me to keep going when things became difficult."*

Christmas cards and postcards to a young college girl!

Rose Watson went outside her own world and received many, many people into her life, and she entered their lives, too. She never built her own private kingdom.

Another thing that makes it hard for the rich to enter the kingdom of God is the care of it all. The race with inflation is a bigger race for the rich. The danger of bad investments is a bigger one, too. So is the problem of protecting one's wealth from deception, fraud, or bad luck. The care of it all can easily become a consuming interest. Black Monday becomes more of a benchmark than Good Friday.

It's like a friend of mine who had a very expensive foreign car. When you went with him to a ballgame, his biggest concern was where to park the car, and he spent most of the time during the game worrying about his car.

Rose Watson didn't do that. She was light-hearted, and worried more about people than anything else in the world. She knew a lot about finance – from the day she studied accounting as a young woman.

She wasn't oblivious to the hard realities of the world of finance, and she wasn't irresponsible about it. But she didn't worry about it with a heavy heart. Rather, she chose to invest her heart somewhere else.

I was particularly struck by a paragraph in one letter: *"I'm sure that God continues to bless you for your spirit of poverty . . . your willingness to share of your own resources, both material and spiritual. You are a true sign to the youth that people do care for them and are willing to invest their time in their formation."*

Rose Watson knew well where to put her heart.

There is one other difficulty that makes it hard for the rich to enter the kingdom of God, and I think it is the greatest difficulty of all. The rich person is well situated in this present order of things, and the kingdom of God can be a terrible threat because it is very "disordering:"

- The last are first and first are last.
- The mighty are pulled down from their thrones, and the lowly are raised up to high places.
- The least is the greatest. The gentle inherit the land.
- The child in the manger is the Messiah . . . the foot washer is the King of Kings . . . the helpless figure on the cross is the Lord of all.

What do we do when the established order of our lives comes face-to-face with the different order of the kingdom of God?

Rose Watson must have faced that same temptation. She must have faced it early and forcefully, for the struggle never showed. Her faith was at the center of her life, and everything else was built around it. The letters in these albums are not written to a humanitarian; they are written to a believer, a disciple of the Lord, who did everything she did because she believed in God.

There are many stories that could be told about Rose Watson. But the greatest story, I believe, is the simple story of a woman who handled well the rich person's journey through the eye of the needle.

In doing so, she reminded us that the journey is ours. For we, too, are the rich who must be careful not to live in our own closed world, who must see that our hearts are invested in the kingdom, who must welcome the "dis-order" of God into the established order we so dearly want to protect.

That is the story we need to hear.

Funeral Mass for Rose E. Watson, Saginaw philanthropist; March 1988.

Msgr. Clem Kern

C lem Kern was one of those people who had this depth of holiness that enabled him to go beyond the categories.

He defied description. A friend of mine tried to do a Myers-Briggs Personality Indicator Test on him and said, "He's the whole thing – he's the whole thing. It's all been integrated – the best of all."

There is something about ministry that requires us to go beyond the categories, whatever they are. Clem Kern was at St. John's Seminary when I was there. I'm the guy that talked him into coming there. You have to understand – he was a little guy and a nice guy and a quiet guy, and everybody loved him.

Well, Clem Kern was asked by this family whose daughter (not young) was going to enter – obviously – a very bad marriage from every point of view, in terms of every category including religion, to talk her out of it.

He told me he was going to do that, so when he came back that night, I said, "How did it go?"

He said, "Well, it didn't work, so I went and talked to the parents."

Of course, the big issue was whether they were going to go to the wedding, which was going to be outside of all the categories, including the Church. And I couldn't wait to hear the answer.

I said, "What did you tell them?"

He said, "Of course, you're going. Don't you be mean to her . . . don't you be mean to her."

Now in some way and somehow, that taught me what going beyond the categories means. Because he didn't say, "Scuttle Church law; forget the categories – they're silly, they're stupid." He went beyond them. He said something that none of us could quibble with: "Don't you be mean to her."

Clem Kern was somebody who was beloved in his parish and by the movers and doers and corporate leaders of the Detroit area – the people with the big bucks who helped him run his poor parish. He was also the big friend of all the unions. Now how he could blend those two I never understood.

When the Playboy Club in Detroit was not treating "bunnies" [the female wait staff] fairly in their wages and the women picketed, Clem Kern went out and picketed with them. Television cameras were there and the television interviewers said aghast: "How can you, a priest, be with these people who dress immodestly?"

Clem said, in his simple, beyond the category way: "I'm for modesty; I'm also for fair wages."

And that was the end of the interview.

It's also how Clem Kern could be with the poor – I mean the down-and-out, the rotten, undeserving poor. But every year he'd also take a group of priests for a vacation in Acapulco. Then, when times changed, he made room for some of the priests' wives. Beyond the categories.

He never made light of the categories. He never said, "It's silly, stupid to observe them." But he could go beyond them.

On the day Jimmy Hoffa was going to jail, Clem Kern said a special Mass for him at Most Holy Trinity Parish in Detroit. The TV cameras were there, and people said, "How can you have a public Mass for this criminal?"

He said, "Well, you see, the best thing we do and the best thing we know how to do is pray for people . . . and Jimmy needs our prayers."

I brought Clem Kern to the seminary so that we could all watch him, and we found out that he did what he did by never doing anything big. In other words, he did things that every one of us can do.

This is my last story. I'm sitting there at St. John's Seminary on a Sunday afternoon. I'm tired and the ballgame is on. I get a call from a person who needs some money . . . and he's lying. He gives me this story that is obviously not true, and I tell him, "Look, I know that you're not telling the truth so thank you and good-bye."

At 11 p.m., I was outside for a breath of fresh air and there came Clem Kern, who was on his way out the door. I asked where he was going and he said, "Well, there's this fellow who just called from a White Castle down in Detroit, and he needs some money because . . ."

As he told this story, I said, "Clem, he's a fake. You're not taken in by that line, are you?"

He said, "Of course not, but I've got to get down there and give him some money and tell him to stop bothering all these priests on the phone."

I stood there and watched the lights of Clem's car trail off in the distance. I was 43 and he was 73, and there he was headed to Detroit at midnight on a "useless mission."

Right then I realized the difference between greatness and high mediocrity.

Commissioning of lay ministers; August 19, 1983.

Consumer mentality

C oming down the elevator in the Hyatt Regency Hotel in Chicago last Friday, a gentleman was mumbling something or other. He turned to me and said, "Well, this is the last time the Hyatt chain is going to see me."

I said, "Oh …" (always looking to hear complaints!).

He said, "Yeah, you know this plastic card they give you to open your door? Well, ours didn't work, and my wife went to get hers changed and, of course, they fixed it, but then when I came back, mine, of course, wouldn't work either. And we're having trouble with it today. So that's it."

I thought of all the things that this monstrous hotel had, all the services and things that are going on here, and some hotel clerk at check-out time is going to have to turn the other cheek because this man was ticked over the plastic card that didn't work well on the door.

That, for me, was a miniature of something that is very much in our culture these days. I'm not sure if I have the word to describe it, but I think you know what I mean. I guess it's connected with a "consumer mentality" that gives us a sense of feeling important enough to write off a whole corporation or write off another person because something they do doesn't measure up to our standards or we found it unsatisfactory.

I always have great admiration for parents when they're going through the phase of raising teenagers. Parents absorb an awful lot of this criticism, especially when teenagers are in their "grouch phase" and the "write-off-everybody-else" phase. Watching that happen, watching my brothers and sisters raise their kids, and watching other friends, I have tremendous admiration for them.

Priests, too, stand for the Church, and get more of this sort of thing today. The priest can be the lightning rod – just like the poor hotel clerk at check-out was going to be the one to get criticized for the plastic card that didn't work.

It's not so much a problem caused by the Church – it's part of our culture, and our Church is set in this culture. It's one of those things that goes on all the time.

And it's one of the hard things about being a waiter, being a servant, being a shepherd.

Saginaw diocesan priests' jubilee; Mt 5:38-42; June 19, 1995.

'Say what you want to say'

*A*s a young priest in Detroit, I was the one who had to get in front of the television cameras when all the changes were breaking in the Church – meat on Friday and all those kinds of things. I was the one who had to answer the reporters' questions.

A crusty old newsman got me aside one time and said, "I can help you out on how to do this. Reporters' questions are often questions that are simply things that are curiosity pieces, and things that they find interesting and not necessarily important. What you should do is use the opportunity of the question to say what you want to say – you don't have to answer the question. Just say what you think you want to say in this golden opportunity."

And he taught me how to do that.

What was asked of Jesus is like a TV reporter's question, a curiosity piece: "Jesus, you've been teaching about this 'kingdom of God.' I've got a question for you: Is it going to be a lot of people or just a few people who get in?"

And Jesus said, "Well, that's an interesting question but I'll tell you what's important is that you don't drift into this kingdom" (and he used the analogy of the narrow door).

I'll tell you something else that's important. This takes some decisions along the way. You can't just keep putting those off (Jesus uses the image of the closed door – it doesn't just stay open). It takes more than a superficial acquaintance with God for me to get into the kingdom.

If I were to sail a small boat across the Atlantic, the same thing would be true. You don't just drift across the Atlantic. It doesn't happen. It takes a lot of work, and along the way you have to make a lot of decisions. The wind's going to blow you off course, the tides, maybe some problems with the equipment, and you can't just keep putting those off because you could drift so far off course that you don't have the food or the fuel to get there. It takes more than a superficial acquaintance with boats and navigation to do that.

I have to ask myself in relationship with God, "Am I just more or less drifting?"

Someone might say, "Well, you're a bishop."

Jesus said, "Let me tell you something: Some who are last are going to be first, and some who are first are going to be last. You never take this for granted."

In relationship to God, am I just more or less drifting, feeling I'll get there? Are there some decisions that I don't face, that I'm putting off, that I ought to make in order to be the person that I know I ought to be?

I also have to ask myself the question: How real is my relationship with Jesus? Is it superficial? Because of my relationship with Jesus, what's different about the way I talk, about the way I act, about the way I think?

Twenty-first Sunday in Ordinary Time/C cycle; Lk 13:22-30; St. Mark Parish in Au Gres.

A shepherd's eye

I had a phone conversation with a friend of mine who is out in north Arizona on a Hopi Indian reservation, where she works helping Native-Americans.

She was telling me what a beautiful attitude they have toward creation, toward the world, toward people. They believe in the Great Spirit, that the Great Spirit fills all things, and we are all part of it together.

The lake is their sister, their brother.

The animals, the flowers, the trees, the sky, the stars – we're all in this together and it is ours. You have this wonderful feeling of being part of the whole of creation – never lonely, never a fragment, but part of the wonder of all creation, of all people.

As she went on, I said, "That's what we teach. That's very much part of our Christian heritage." We believe that human beings were made to tell the story of how God took the clay of the earth – we're connected with the earth. We talk of the "cosmic Christ" – Jesus who came to be part of all creation. The Psalms say, "The earth is the Lord's and all who dwell in it." Jesus taught that whatever you do for the littlest one, you do it to him. We talk about the "body of Christ," how we all are together.

And I went on, talking about how we believe that.

She said, "Then why don't you teach it more?"

So I told her to mind her own business! (I really didn't.)

I said, "Well, maybe we ought to. Maybe, stop to think of it, we spend our time talking about more internal things – about what you have to do to be a member of the Church and things like that which you have to take care of. We talk about the details and forget to talk about the whole thing . . . the wonderful beauty of our teachings . . . about God and about Christ who became part of creation, and how we are all part of it."

In the Gospel, Jesus talks about being a shepherd. A shepherd's staff is a bishop's staff and the symbolism is that the bishop is supposed to be a good shepherd. (I really have a shepherd's staff, by the way. I got it from a sheep farm in Idaho. It cost $12, but then I broke it down into three parts so that I can take it in my car without it sticking out the window.) When I look upon my staff as part of me, and myself as part of all people and all creation, it's different because something that you're not part of, that's not yours, you treat differently.

I admit that I don't take as good care of a rented car as I do my own. That's just the way it is. This earth is no "rented car." The people on this earth are not strangers. They are our sisters and brothers. The earth is God's, as are all who dwell in it. We, like God whose Spirit is within us, are to care for it, all people in this earth, and nurture it.

Everybody is called to be a shepherd of this world. If you look at this earth with a shepherd's eye, it will look different and we will act differently.

We can leave out no country, no people. We care about the cities. We care about the earth. We care about the people. We are shepherds, not hired hands. We don't work for pay. We are God's daughters . . . God's sons. The Spirit of God is within us.

The Lord is all creation, and all people in it and we are part of this wondrous creation, and placed here by God to continue his shepherding work.

Fourth Sunday of Easter/B cycle; Jn 10:11-18; confirmation at St. Agnes Parish in Pinconning, St. Mary Parish in Nine Mile, and St. Michael Parish in Port Austin.

Trappist monks

$\mathcal{A}$ couple of years ago, I gave a retreat for the monks in a Trappist monastery in California.

Trappists are monks who live an extremely ascetical life and who, among other things, observe perpetual silence. They only speak to pray . . . and also in necessary situations. In most 24-hour days, they speak aloud not a word, except to pray.

These monks live in the Benedictine tradition, which is summarized in the Latin phrase, "ora et labora," which means "prayer and work." They earn their own way by working, and they pray day and night.

In this particular Trappist monastery, their work was cultivating walnut trees and plum trees. They lived on vast acreage with thousands of walnut trees and plum trees – the kind of plum trees that produced fruit that was especially good for prunes. That is how they made their living.

In the course of the eight-day retreat, I got to know one of the older monks whose specialty was pruning the plum trees. There were thousands of them, and he spent all day out there every day deciding which branches were the ones that should be pruned in order to make the tree more capable of producing good plums.

He was their expert "pruner." A machine can't do what he did. You have to look over the tree and decide what's best for the tree, and then do the pruning that helps the tree.

I used to walk out there in the afternoon while he was working and watch him at work. We became good friends – he could talk to me because I was the retreat master.

One day, after we had gotten to know each other pretty well, I said to him, "You must be able to do a lot of praying and feel very close to God when you're working out in the peace and quiet of this orchard.

He stopped and (I remember the moment well) a tear crept into his eye as he said, "Oh, indeed I do. I love these trees and I know them well. I always think of John's Gospel when Jesus talks about the fact that he is the vine and we are the branches, and that the Father prunes away the branches that are in the way.

"While I'm pruning, I say to the Lord, 'Thanks for doing that to me. You have pruned me, and shaped me, and helped me become what I never could have become without you. I'm not perfect, and I know I need more pruning, but you are always there to make me more into your image.'

"The Lord has done wonderful things for me, and I'd be nowhere without that pruning."

I've never forgotten what the monk said.

I hope I can be more conscious of it, and thank God, like that old monk did. Even if there is some suffering in my life, God can turn it into something helpful.

God is always taking care of us, and doing some pruning, and shaping us more in his own image.

Thank you, God, for taking such good care of me, in ways I don't even realize. You've been good to me and I'd be nowhere without you.

It's a good prayer, and I learned it from that monk.

Fifth Sunday of Easter; May 21, 2000; Jn 15:1-8.

Gift of faith

_____

I was talking to a priest a couple of days ago, and I consider him a wise person.

I was talking about how to get people more involved or more alive in their faith, about things that we could do in parishes or in the diocese that would just get Catholic people more alive.

He said to me (and I'll never forget this), "You can't do anything. It's a gift, a gift of faith. You either have it or you don't."

He said, "I was just dealing with somebody whose wife was dying of cancer – young – and I talked to him and he was trying to make sense out of it. I told him, 'I can give you all kinds of ideas and I can tell you about the suffering Jesus, but I can't explain it to you. You just have to believe that *somehow* God's going to make sense out of this whole thing and *somehow* it's not useless and *somehow* it's not awful. That *somehow* – that's faith, and that's a gift.'"

Now that's something I learned in the second grade. But as he sat there and said it (and as I thought about my own experience as a priest), I thought: That's true.

We can do good liturgy – and we ought to – and we can do good religious education, and we ought to. We can do lots of things. But we know (and we all learned this early): Faith is a gift.

If you've got the gift, then you love the Church and you have a conviction about what you're doing, even though you don't always understand. And life (and death, too) somehow can seem to make sense.

But I can't explain it.

It's a gift.

You either have it or you don't. Logic helps. Theology helps. Religious education helps. But they only help. You either have it or you don't.

Ascension/A cycle; Mt 28:16-20.

Lines we draw

Our Diocesan Council gathered and asked some Hispanic leaders in the diocese to spend two-and-a-half hours with us and tell us about their concerns and their needs, and ways in which we aren't responding.

They talked about things that we've all heard: More inclusion in the liturgy, more Spanish culture, more representation on diocesan boards, more representation among diocesan and parish employees.

After the meeting, after everyone had gone home, I was talking to a Hispanic woman, the mother of six children. I was trying to talk about some of these things and I was talking about them with my own logic.

She said, "You don't understand."

Of course, that's all I have to hear – "you don't understand" – once again.

So I said, "Well, tell me why I don't understand."

She said: "Well, let me put it this way. Everything's fine while my children are growing up. Now my daughter has turned 17 and she found out that she can't date a white man. My other daughter is 13 and she doesn't know that yet, but she's going to find out."

I said, "Now I understand."

That's the issue. The lines we draw that divide people.

We can't change social patterns all around us, but within the Church those social patterns cannot be tolerated. Without intending it, that social pattern can be in the Church. This can be our Church . . . and not quite yours. This can be our diocese . . . and not quite yours. This can be our parish . . . and not quite yours.

We draw that line of "not quite" in lots of different ways. It's not just Hispanic and Anglo. It's black and white. It's nationalities. It can be between clergy and laity. It can be between man and woman. It can be between religious women and the rest of the Church. It can be between one parish and another parish. It can be between groups within a parish.

It can be between people who are sinners but their sins are not known and people who are sinners and their sins are known. It can be between winners and losers. It can be between refined and unrefined. It can be between contributors and non-contributors.

We draw the line in lots of different ways – and we all do it. It's subtle.

We should be the strangest collection of people the world has ever seen, who can come together, even though we can't change all the social patterns around us.

Chrism Mass; Lk 4:16-21; April 17, 1984.

Part VI
The other day I had to go out of town . . .

The other day I had to go out of town . . .

—⬭—

Ken Untener quickly discovered that something can happen when you become a bishop. "You can start to act differently and in a way that's not entirely good," he said. "You dress differently . . . You can easily be the center of attention.

"It's like carbon monoxide. You don't know it's happening. You live in a higher realm. You're in a more protected realm. You have a house that doesn't have the normal traffic of parish life. You have someone answer the phone for you, and people address you with a special title.

"So, a few months into that, I noticed that I was acting differently and I was taking on a role rather than being myself. I also had a friend or two who told me, in a not complimentary way, that I was acting differently."

He decided to live a more normal life, "to breathe the air of parish life."

Within three months of becoming bishop of Saginaw in 1980, Ken announced he would sell the three-story 23-room bishop's mansion where his predecessors had lived. He would become a perpetual houseguest, a "professional sponger," taking turns living at rectories or homes across the diocese.

Throughout his 24 years as bishop, he moved 69 times, finding a new home every two or three months. Occasionally he would house sit. Once he lived with the local Episcopal bishop and his wife. Another time he stayed in a small, unused hospital room at St. Mary's Medical Center in downtown Saginaw.

As he traveled from parish to parish, his possessions fit inside three duffle bags, several garment bags and two small canvas bags. His bishop's crosier could be taken apart into three pieces that fit inside a duffle bag.

"If it's not in my trunk, it's not worth saving," he'd say. He drove his Chevrolet Corsica 40,000 miles a year, visiting parishes, giving talks, making hospital visits. On those visits, he usually wore a light gray clerical shirt and a sweater or a well-worn gray corduroy jacket.

Wherever he lived, he ate what his hosts ate, did his own laundry, had lunch with parishioners and staff, and helped out with weekday Masses (when his schedule permitted). He got to know the priests and the people they served – "I get to soak up what is in the air."

"What I'm trying to do," he told an interviewer in 1982, "is change the idea that the chancery is the source. It's a resource, not head-quarters from which plans and programs flow out to branch offices. It cannot pretend to know everything and to control what parishes do. It should help parishes, enable them to do better the creative things they are already doing."

His travel wasn't limited to the diocese's 11 counties. As his rep-utation as a speaker and retreat master grew, he received invitations to speak throughout the United States and around the world, traveling to Australia, Europe, Asia, the Middle East, and Central America.

As rector of St. John's Seminary, he had introduced an annual program for seminarians to study in the Holy Land. The year that he was scheduled to lead that trip, he was named bishop of Saginaw and didn't have a chance to go. That changed in 1993, when he led a group of priests, religious, and laity on the first diocesan visit to the Holy Land. It was a trip he was to repeat many times.

No matter how long his trip was or where his travels took him, Ken prided himself on never having to check luggage at an airport.

He just carried his own duffle bag.

The Lord on my side

About a month ago, with the airports a mess now because of all the security, I was going to miss my plane.

I had an electronic ticket and the line was way too long to go to the ticket counter.

So, since I was going to miss my plane, I decided to try electronic check-in. I had never done an electronic check-in before, and I didn't know how to do it.

I'm standing there and this older woman said, "You want me to help you?"

I said, "I've never done this."

She said, "I'll go with you."

I don't know what she was there for. She wasn't an airline employee.

She said, "I'll go with you," and then, "Okay, now punch that. Now push that. Now do you want . . . ?" and she did it for me.

Well, I was just about to miss my plane. It meant so much to me when she said that she would help me because I'd have been there for an hour trying to figure it out by myself.

She may be my angel.

That's the way Jesus says, "I'll be with you." Jesus said, "I will send my spirit upon you to be with you."

I can't see Jesus, but Jesus is with me as close as that nice woman was. As close as anyone is when they say, "Come on, take my hand and I'll go with you."

Even when I'm all alone and there's no one else there who's on my side, I know that the Lord is with me. My heart is strong and I've got courage.

Religious Education Mass at St. Vincent de Paul Parish, Bay City; Lk 21:12-19; November 28, 2001.

The free ticket

---

*T*oward the end of last year, I had accumulated enough miles on an airline to get one of those free tickets. So I made plans for a one-day trip to visit someone.

I made the reservations in advance, and on the day of the flight went to the airport.

Since I didn't have any baggage to check, I went directly to the gate and waited in line. When my turn came, I handed my ticket to the agent and said, "I'd like a window seat in the non-smoking section."

He looked at the ticket, handed it back, and said, "This ticket is no good."

I said, "What do you mean – no good? It says this free flight is valid for six more months."

He said, "Yes, but it also says that you can't use it during the Christmas season – which started yesterday."

There it was, right there in the list of conditions, and I hadn't noticed it.

I took my ticket and went home.

We've all received a free ticket from the Lord – a free ticket for forgiveness. We can use it over and over again, and we get forgiveness. It is a free ticket. We could never afford it, and, as a matter of fact, we don't have to pay one thing for it. The Lord gives it to us as a gift. We need that ticket and we will need it more than ever at the end of our life when we stand before God.

That is the picture that came to my mind when I thought about what happened at the airport.

In my fantasy, I picture myself turning in the free ticket of forgiveness at the gate and the Lord saying, "This ticket is no good."

I would say, "What do you mean, it's no good? It says that you forgive everything for free, and it says that you have forgiven anything along the way whenever I said I was sorry, and that it could be used over and over again (which I did)."

Then I picture the Lord saying, "Yes, but it also says that it is only good if you forgive others the same way. You haven't been doing that, and this ticket is no good."

A fantasy like that makes me think . . . and think hard.

Twenty-fourth Sunday in Ordinary Time/A cycle; Televised Mass for Shut-ins; September 13, 1987.

Good news and the bad news

I remember vividly an incident that occurred on the day when the air controllers' strike was supposed to go into effect at midnight.

It was Sunday evening and I was on a DC-10 from out west going to Chicago. The strike was supposed to go into effect at midnight, and everyone was hurrying to make it back home.

The flight went routinely enough for a couple hours, and then the captain came on the speaker and said that there was a back-up of air traffic in Chicago. We didn't have enough fuel to circle for the amount of time necessary, so we would have to go to Kansas City for refueling. That meant going quite a bit out of our way and also a long delay that would cause many of us to miss our connections in Chicago.

With the imminent strike, many of us expected to be marooned.

As if that weren't enough, once we landed and arrived at the gate, the stewardess came on the speaker and said there weren't enough personnel in the airport, so we would not be allowed to get off the airplane.

This really caused a stir because a number of people wanted to phone their families to say that they would be missing their connections.

The mood inside the plane grew surly, and then all kinds of rumors started.

People were saying that large planes like this could fly the Pacific Ocean, so why couldn't they make it to Chicago? Others said that they didn't see any fuel trucks out there, so they didn't believe this business about refueling.

A number of people were crowding around the exit and arguing with the stewardess. I happened to be in that area and, although I had no reason to have to call anyone, I entered the discussion.

I asked her why we couldn't get off, even though there weren't enough gate personnel. She said that it would be too difficult to round the people up when it was time for the plane to leave.

I asked what would happen if we took it as our own responsibility and left the plane only with the understanding that we did so at our own risk.

She didn't have much to say to that, and that was all it took for the group to storm the jetway and head for the terminal.

I felt like I had led a mutiny.

As I was standing there, enjoying a soft drink, the pilot came by and I began to chat with him. I asked him some of the questions that I had heard asked. Like, why a plane like this wouldn't have enough fuel?

He explained that it was a very hot day and that the temperatures on the runway when we took off were probably around 110 or 120 degrees. Since a jet engine is made to function at 30 or 40 degrees below zero, it does not run very effectively at high temperatures. Furthermore, the plane was very full because of everyone's anxiety about the strike. For that reason, he took on less fuel than he normally would, to reduce the weight on take-off.

He had checked with Chicago and the weather seemed fine, and there were no apparent tie-ups. However, as the day wore on (and after we were already in flight), the air controllers apparently started to space out the traffic a bit more. When you do that at the busiest airport in the world, you very quickly have a backlog of planes that will have to circle for 40 or 50 minutes.

As soon as he got word about that, he realized that we would have to take on more fuel, so he diverted the flight to Kansas City.

It made perfect good sense and now I understood.

I said to myself, "Why didn't he just tell the people?"

Information builds trust; lack of information breeds suspicion and rumors. It convinced me of something I already believed in, namely, that it is best to tell people everything – the good news and the bad news.

That is one of my operating principles.

Talk to diocesan employees; August 17, 1981.

Parking ticket

---

*T*he other day I had to go out of town for a three-day meeting.

As I was driving into the airport (a little bit late for my plane), I drove into the parking lot and there was an automatic gate that opens when you take out your ticket from the machine. The ticket registers what time you went in.

When I arrived, it was in the middle of a thunderstorm and someone apparently blinded by the rain had driven through the gate, and it was broken and lying on the ground. As a result, the machine would not cough up any ticket for me.

I was late so I just went in. That was on Wednesday night.

On Saturday night when I returned, I drove to the cashier's window and I told the woman mistakenly that I had come on Thursday night, and I explained the circumstances.

She routinely wrote up a form and told me to sign it and she would charge me just for that.

Then it dawned on me that I had actually come on Wednesday. So I stopped and asked her to rewrite it so that I would pay what I actually owed.

As she was doing that, I thought to myself: That just cost me five bucks. There would be no return on that. The people at the parking lot wouldn't admire me or be my friends. I would never see the same people again. I had no wonderful feeling inside that they needed the money. It simply cost me five bucks.

It costs to be honest.

Goodness costs.

Seventeenth Sunday in Ordinary Time/A cycle; Mt 13:44-52.

Giving the gift of life

A while back, I was quite a ways from Saginaw in my car. It was a little after midnight, and my car went dead.

I got it to a gas station, and the fellow there worked hard on it for over an hour, but we couldn't bring it to life. Finally he said that he had done about everything he could, and I would have to take it to a dealer in the morning and see what they could do.

There I was, on this very cold night, in the middle of nowhere, with a car that was dead.

I had worked in a gas station myself back in high school, so I suggested that we try one more thing: We put a couple of cans of dry gas in the gas tank, and then shook it up pretty good. Then we put about a cup full of gas in the carburetor and, since by then the battery was dead, we hooked up some jumper cables, and gave it a try.

It worked! What a moment when that engine came alive. It's a great thing to be there when that happens.

It is even a greater sensation to see a new surge of life in a human being.

I lived by the water back in my early days, and I saw a lot of people pulled out of the water after going under a couple of times. When you give someone mouth-to-mouth resuscitation, or pound on their chest, and suddenly they start to breathe and their heart starts to beat – it is a great moment. It is a moment of giving life.

On the other end of it, I remember watching my sister die.

It happened a couple of years ago. She had been sick for quite some time, and I saw her die. It was hard, and I would have done anything to be able to give her life. But it was not to be. I remember sitting there during her last days and thinking of all the ways that I could have given her life years earlier. By that I mean, I could have brought more life to her when she was alive.

She had been sick for a long time, and I know that at times she was down and lonely. It would have been so easy for me to give her a call, or stop by, or get a couple of people together to do something special and bring some freshness to her life.

I thought of all the ways I could have been a better life giver, and I promised myself that from now on I would try to be a life giver whenever or wherever I could. I promised myself that I wouldn't pass up chances like that ever again. I would try to bring life to friends, to enemies, to strangers I meet over the counter at the store or at the gas station, or to people who write me letters – to anybody and everybody I could.

When I think about the moment when my car came to life on that cold night . . . when I think about people brought back to life from the brink of drowning . . . when I think about all the ways I could have given my sister more life – I realize what a great gift it is to give the gift of life.

Sixth Sunday of Easter/B cycle; Jn 15:7-17.

Ellis Island

_____

When I was in New York, I made it a point to visit Ellis Island – a 15-minute boat ride out toward the sea, near the Statue of Liberty.

They've restored the buildings where so many immigrants were processed and there were some excellent displays. Let me tell you, it's something to stand on that island and think back to what our grandparents or great-grandparents experienced in that same place.

There was a half-hour film presentation spliced together from old footage, photographs, and the voices of people who once came through Ellis Island. They had left everything behind in their homeland. Some came alone to prepare the way for the rest of their families. Others came as families with little children.

Some traveled first- or second-class. They had it pretty easy, and, when they got here, were given preferential treatment.

But most traveled in steerage and faced a two- or three-week voyage, crowded together in the hold of the ship which, within a day or two after setting sail, was squalor – people getting seasick, very few bathroom facilities.

Getting here was only part of the problem. Once they arrived, they were taken to Ellis Island to see if they would be allowed into our country. You know what it's like in an airlines terminal at the crowded gate when the plane is delayed. Well, this was a hundred times worse. They didn't know where they were supposed to go, what they were supposed to do . . . they didn't speak the language . . . and it took forever as one by one they were checked to see if they would be turned away because of their health or lack of employable skills or lack of money. Their status in their own country didn't matter. They had no status here, no connections, no preferential treatment, nothing to fall back on.

Some were sent back to where they came from. Others were allowed in, and you can imagine their feelings when at long last they were put on a boat and brought to the mainland of the United States of America.

Because of my trip to Ellis Island, I have a far deeper appreciation of what I can so easily take for granted in this country into which I was born. I wish everyone could see that film, especially young people.

I stayed for a while on Ellis Island and walked around. There came upon me an experience I don't know if I can describe.

I pictured these immigrants arriving frightened, alone, with only one sack that held all their possessions. It became for me an image of what it could be like when we die and arrive in a "new world" – alone, frightened, with *none* of our possessions, no special status, no preferential treatment.

Our status before death no longer matters – whether we were rich or poor, whether we had a lot of connections or had none, whether we were famous or unknown, educated or uneducated. Whether you were a doctor, lawyer, CEO, or bishop no longer mattered. Here you were in a new world where the last will be first and the first last.

It's simply an image but it makes you think.

Death doesn't have to be like Ellis Island. We don't have to come to the "new world" as strangers. The Lord will be there to receive us and walk us through death.

Thirteenth Sunday in Ordinary Time/B cycle; July 2, 2000; Mk 5:21-43.

This little light

---

*I*n 1989, I was in Menlo Park, California, just south of San Francisco, when the great earthquake hit – the most recent large earthquake in that area at that time.

It hit about five o'clock in the afternoon.

I was making some presentations to a group of priests who had gathered at the seminary there, and when it hit, we all got out of the building as fast as we could. I had never been in an earthquake, but they had. They knew that the first thing you do is get out of any large building in case it collapses (like the Twin Towers).

So there we were, all standing outside. We saw the power lines flashing – the electricity was out everywhere. We heard sirens everywhere, and we just waited to see what would happen.

They knew there would be aftershocks, and sometimes a building that had been weakened by the earthquake could come down because of one of the aftershocks. And the aftershocks came, and the large building where we were staying still stood.

It began to get dark – very, very dark because there was no electricity anywhere. Hours later – it was maybe 10 p.m. that night – some said we may as well go back into the darkened building and try to get some sleep, and if we felt an aftershock, we should get out right away.

Well, I was a stranger to this place. I didn't know if I could find my room in total darkness. Or if I did find it, I didn't know if I could get out if there was a major aftershock. I was wondering about this when a priest came over to me. He had this little key chain with a small light on it. If you squeezed it, this little light shone. I still have it – I keep it in my center desk drawer as a memento. It still works.

It's really only a small glow, a dim light, not what you'd call the beam of a flashlight. But let me tell you, this little light meant everything to me that night. I could find my way to my room, and I knew that I could get out of my room if I had to. For me, this little light helped to overcome the "evil" of the great earthquake.

I don't keep many mementos. But I kept this one. It's always reminded me of that simple song: *"This little light of mine, I'm going to let it shine . . . let it shine, let it shine, let it shine."*

So I should never say, "My light isn't bright enough." Jesus didn't ask us to be great searchlights reaching into the sky for miles. He only asked that we bring light, not darkness, to our world.

We probably should have those words on our bathroom mirror: *"This little light of mine, I'm going to let it shine."*

Fifth Sunday in Ordinary Time/A cycle; January 10, 2002; Mt 5:13-16.

You need a good script

I was down in Cincinnati, Ohio, for a day-and-a-half with the Fountain Square Fools [a liturgical story theater group].

I had been asked to be a narrator on a 20-part videotape that they were making for confirmation preparation, and they brought in an actress to do it along with me (they wanted to spruce it up a little bit, obviously).

It was clearly a case of "rent a bishop . . . rent an actress." She was quite a good actress on Broadway, had appeared on "St. Elsewhere" and "Hill Street Blues," and was on her way to Hollywood to do a movie made for television – I can't think of its name. As a matter of fact, I forget her name.

I had never done anything like that before. I'm used to talking to *live* people – an audience. The script was all written and on the teleprompter, which I was supposed to look at for my lines.

I'll tell you a funny story. The first one to muff a line was the actress. The first scene, we just get into it – and she muffs a line. So I stood up and said, "I can't work with this woman!" At any rate, guess who muffed all the others!

I said to her, as they were fussing, "Give me a two-minute lesson on how to act. I don't know anything about acting. What do you do when you're looking at somebody and you know they know what you're going to say?"

She said, "Here's what you do: You figure out what the meaning of your line is and you try to bring out of the other person whatever effect that line is supposed to have. You figure out what this line is supposed to do to the other person, and you just try to figure out how you would say it in a way that would bring it out of them.

"Just think about that. Don't try to act the line out. Think of what this is supposed to do to the other person. Look them in the eye, and try to make that happen to them.

"That's why you have to have a good script."

The best actor in the world cannot make a bad script good because the lines won't do it. What's happening is not real. An actor is always trying to bring out of the other person what the line is designed to bring, so you have to have a good script.

We Christians have an awfully good script. We have the Gospels and these words are an awfully good script. What we have to do is find whatever way works without footnotes, without acting, to really make those words produce what they were intended to produce in us and in others.

I've got to chew on the words of the Gospels. I've got to re-commit myself to them. I have to see them in a new light, in a fresh light. That's the only way I am going to take this good script of my baptismal commitment, of my ordination commitment, of my commitment when I came to Saginaw, and make it real.

Twenty-sixth Sunday in Ordinary Time/A cycle; Mt. 21:28-32; commissioning of lay ministers; September 27, 1987.

Pearl Harbor Memorial

I was in Honolulu giving a retreat to Army chaplains based in the Pacific.

On the afternoon before leaving, I visited the Pearl Harbor Memorial.

First, there is a 30-minute film presentation, then you go out the back door of the theater right into a boat. It's about a 10-minute ride over to that white memorial structure (you've seen pictures of it) built right over the sunken battleship, the USS Arizona.

You get off there and spend about 15 minutes just looking, looking down at the sunken hull of that battleship and thinking of the 1,700 sailors who died, most of whose remains are still in the ship. Then you sail back to the mainland.

When I first arrived at the site, it was about a half-hour before the film started, so I walked around the area, walking along the shore and reading some of the plaques showing how the harbor looked at the time of the attack and designating certain sites you could see from that point.

I also went into the small museum that had pictures and artifacts – a scale model of the Arizona, pictures actually taken by some of the Japanese pilots during the attack, the shell of a torpedo that had been used.

There were about 75 or 100 people there waiting for the film presentation.

I was walking around for about 10 minutes and suddenly something dawned on me. No one was speaking out loud. There were occasional whispers, but there was a hush throughout the whole area. There were no signs calling for silence. It's just that nobody was speaking, and people walked slowly, even the children.

Then I noticed a small group of Japanese tourists. There were about four or five of them. They were talking in a normal tone, not in a whisper, and they were taking one another's pictures in front of some of the displays. They weren't disrespectful, just acting natural, and not reluctant to smile into the camera.

It was different for them.

Now I had never thought of this before, but it occurred to me then: How are you supposed to act when you visit the *other* country's war memorial?

How *should* Japanese tourists act when they visit Pearl Harbor?

How *should* tourists from northern Vietnam act when they visit the Vietnam Wall in Washington D.C., with all those names on it? Should they stand in front of it and have their picture taken?

How *should* U.S. citizens act when they visit the Japanese memorial at Hiroshima where hundreds of thousands of men, women, and children (civilians) were killed by the atomic bomb? Should we have our picture taken?

How *should* German citizens act when they visit Normandy and see those rows and rows of white crosses, the cemetery where the Allied soldiers are buried?

It was a long flight back home. I flew all night and the plane was half-empty. I was in the back all by myself preparing for the weekend Masses. I read the Gospel where Jesus says to love your enemy, and I thought long thoughts.

It began to come home to me that the way we're going about these things isn't going to work. We kill one another, then build memorials – it's been going on for thousands of years. It's not going to work.

But then I said (as people have said for 20 centuries), "The trouble is, what Jesus says in this Gospel is impossible. You can't live that way in the real world – love your enemies, do good to those who hate you, turn the other cheek, give things away. You can't live that way."

Now I didn't work it all out, but I came up with two reflections:

First, as I was saying to myself, "You can't live that way . . . Jesus couldn't have meant this literally," I saw the problem with saying that. The problem is that if Jesus didn't mean it literally, then why in the world did he *do* it literally? That's what struck me. *Jesus did this.*

I can't say anymore, "It can't be done." Jesus did it, and it was a wonderful thing that he did.

When he was arrested, he healed the ear of one of the men who had come to do him in. "Do good to those who hate you."

When he was on the cross, he forgave the people who were torturing and killing him: "Father, forgive them for they know not what they are doing."

Jesus meant it. He not only said it. He did it.

My second thought was this. It's not as though God is up there counting up whether we're kind to our enemies – keeping a record. The clue to this Gospel is when Jesus said, "If you do this, then . . . you will be children of God, for God is kind to the ungrateful and wicked. Be merciful, just as also your Father is merciful."

Jesus is saying, "You were made to act this way. It's in your genes. You are made in the image and likeness of God, and you'll never be happy any other way."

Jesus was telling us to act this way because it's in us to be this way.

Seventh Sunday in Ordinary Time/C cycle; Lk 6:27-38; February 18, 2001.

Sermon on the Mount

I spent the good part of a week in Cuernavaca, Mexico (about an hour-and-a-half southwest of Mexico City), trying to work on my Spanish at an intensive language school with one-to-one tutoring almost five hours a day.

I lived with a Mexican family who didn't speak English. The first two days, they thought I was a deaf mute. Actually, I learned to get on quite well with one member of the family who was a year-and-a-half old. We both knew about as many words and neither one of us cared how we pronounced them.

Then on Friday of that week, I went to Mexico City. I took a long journey by bus – never really got *out* of the city because the population of Greater Mexico City is 20 million people. I think that's about how many people there are in all of Canada. Mexico City is the biggest city in the world, and it has grown because people are coming into the city when they can't make it anymore out on the land.

A priest that I know who is from Saginaw (and who was ordained the same year as I) has been working with poor people there for more than 10 years, and I traveled out to see him.

It was a journey I shall never forget. I was riding in this vehicle that they call a bus. Once you got outside the center of the city but well within the city, you could see as far as the eye could see on both sides, rows and rows and rows of shacks – barrios – as far as the horizon in both directions, for miles and miles and miles and miles. When I got to the place where the priest was, there were still miles and miles of shacks to be seen.

I spent the day with him, and it was a day that is seared in my memory. I thought there was a stream running by – it's open sewage, which I had never seen before like that.

Toward the end of the day as I was getting ready to go back, I said to him, "Fritz, what's going to change all this? What has to happen for this to change?"

He looked at me (he's a very gentle, soft-spoken person) and he said with utter sincerity, "A complete revolution. Not a violent one – doesn't have to be – but as things are set up now, these millions of people don't have a chance. They don't have access to money or the means to make money, and it's just not going to work until you turn it upside down and reorganize and redistribute."

He said, "I don't expect to live to see that . . . it may take some generations and I don't know how it will happen, and so what I just try to do is to treat them with respect. I work especially hard with the young people and try to give them some values. Every now and then, I bring in a speaker to talk about unions and whatever else. Maybe 20 or 30 people will come, but that's something and I try to plant good seed. Some day, maybe three or four generations from now, it will bear fruit."

When I left there, I had a long ride by myself. I thought about Matthew's Gospel of the Sermon on the Mount. Jesus preaches a revolution. He preaches an upside-down way of looking at things and says, "Blest are the poor and blest are the sorrowing, and the peacemakers and the gentle, and blest are you when they persecute you for trying to do what I have called you to do." He talks in that whole Sermon on the Mount about the revolutionary charter of the kingdom. He talks about how you look at and treat people.

I thought to myself, "Ken, you've got to learn something from Fritz. Stop worrying about how it's all going to work out and being very selective about how you live the Gospel. Just treat everybody with respect, and live every day by the revolutionary teachings of the Sermon on the Mount.

"Just plant good seed as Fritz was doing with these thousands and thousands of people. It's the Lord who builds the house. It's the Lord who gives growth. Live the Gospel and be peaceful and happy about that and really treat people – all people, people you don't know and will never see again – the way the Lord taught us to treat people. And you are living the revolution that is the Gospel."

I'll tell you what the deep-down decision is that makes you a follower of Christ. It's to believe in what Jesus said about the way you treat people. It will change the way you act every day, and it will cause the quiet and gradual revolution that one day will produce the kingdom of God."

Sixth Sunday in Ordinary Time/A cycle; Mt 5:17-37; St. Mary's University Parish, Mt. Pleasant; February 10-11, 1990.

'Family' toward the poor of the world

I was in Mexico City for a conference, and I can tell you firsthand (I've been there twice before) that the living conditions in most of that city are like the slums in our city.

During the conference, I learned an astounding fact. I learned that the country with the most billionaires is the United States (no surprise there), the second is Japan, the third is Germany, and the fourth is Mexico.

Fourth in the whole world, and you see so many, many people living in conditions that make you want to cry.

Well, if some extraterrestrial visitors would visit places like that in the United States, in Mexico, and much, much worse in some other countries, they would say to us, "You let that happen? You let that go on? You call this a civilized society? You sleep at night knowing that there are millions of people like that on your planet? Why, it's as primitive as infant sacrifice. How does that happen?"

Now, understand, I don't have an instant political or sociological solution. All I know is that this is the condition of our planet, and we do let it go on.

What would we say to these extraterrestrial visitors?

Perhaps some might say, "Well, we do our best and we'd like to be different, but you have to understand that for some of those people, it's their own fault. A lot of them really could do better if they made some effort."

I thought about that, then something struck me.

I come from a large family – nine children. I remember, now that I think about it, how often family members had to fall back on the family.

The economic level of my family was lower middle class. We didn't have a big house but I remember, now that I look back, that some of my older brothers and sisters, after they had been married for a few years, came back to live with us for a time. They needed some "temporary help" in a difficult time, or a time of transition, and we just took them in.

I remember other situations where the family helped each of us when there was some kind of problem – the loss of a job, health problems. We had family to fall back on.

The question wasn't: Which ones will we help?

The question was: Are we going to be "family" toward family members?

What struck me was this: a good part of the world (including people in our own country) don't have a family to fall back on. Or, if they do, the family is in the same predicament and can't give them the help they need.

The response of Jesus to the question, "Who is my neighbor?" turns the question around. Jesus says, "Stop worrying about categorizing people by asking 'Who is my neighbor?' and discover that you are supposed to be 'family' to other people, to the whole world."

Fifteenth Sunday in Ordinary Time/C cycle; Lk 10:25-37; July 15, 2001.

Words, words

I made a trip to Stratford, Ontario, and saw two of Shakespeare's plays, "Richard II" and "Henry IV Part One."

We went fairly early in the morning and came back late the same night. On the way there, we studied the plays together and learned a lot about Shakespeare. How he had a way with words!

Did you know that in his plays, he uses more than 17,000 different words? The normal vocabulary we use is around 800 words. We all know the *meaning* of a lot more words, but the words we use when we speak in conversation, or in sermons, or in bulletin articles, or in letters – these words are rather limited.

Shakespeare uses *17,000* different words. These aren't big words. They were taken from farming or from the tavern or from pain or from love. They are words that are concrete and rich and full and taken from real life.

When we saw the plays, we appreciated all this. We had read the plays in advance and when the speakers made those words come even more alive, we drank them in and enjoyed every drop.

When I got back and was at my desk working the next day, I was writing letters and preparing a homily for Sunday. I thought to myself, "You can do better with words."

I thought about how Shakespeare had chosen such concrete and rich words, so I summoned my resources and I wrote better that day. I just didn't want to write letters that were bland or sermons filled with clichés. Shakespeare had moved me to do better with words.

Quality, goodness – these touch other people and affect them. The richness of Shakespeare with the English language on Friday touched me on Saturday, and I'll never forget it. When I just can't get a thought, or I feel bland as I am trying to write something, I will pick up Shakespeare and read him for 10 minutes and his use of the English language will light a fire in me.

Goodness also does that . . . it really does. The life of Jesus is the very best example of this. Look at how his life has touched so many, many other people.

As I thought about all this, I wondered why if goodness so obviously produces good effects, it doesn't inspire all of us to be better, to reach out to others and light a fire with our own goodness?

As I thought about it, I saw three problems:

Goodness doesn't *always* work. I heard someone once say, "No good deed goes unpunished." Sometimes when we try to be helpful and to be good, we are repaid with suspicion, anger, or who knows what else. Everyone has, at times, been hurt by our own good deeds. We are wounded. And (although it sounds funny) we are afraid to be *too* good because there are times when we have been good and we have been hurt.

Our good seed doesn't always bear fruit quickly. One person sows and another reaps. The fire that is lit in the other person does not happen before our eyes. Shakespeare wrote nearly 400 years ago, and it affected me a couple of months ago. If we were talking about the good effects that we have had on one another, we would discover that it was a delayed effect and we never even knew about it. One sows, another reaps.

The goodness that we have, our most precious gifts are not grandiose. I would like to be the architect of the kingdom. I would like to do goodness on a grand scale. In reality, I am called to be a tiny jeweler. I am called to do fine work that will certainly have its effects on the kingdom, but these are the works of a jeweler, not an architect.

Here we are, with so many gifts that could do so much good. People need them. We've got to share them.

That is true ministry.

Fifth Sunday in Ordinary Time/A cycle; Mt 5:13-16.

What the poor deserve

When I was visiting Australia some years ago, I visited the cathedral in Sydney.

They told me this story of how the crusty old archbishop, many years before, had built the cathedral, but had not been able to finish the two towers in the front, because all the money had been spent on the rest of the building. So there was some question as to whether or not the expense was too much. The papal nuncio (who was there on the occasion) did say when he was asked to speak at the Eucharist, that one has to wonder if this money could have been given to the poor.

At the banquet afterwards, the old archbishop said, "I was so surprised to hear on the lips of the papal delegate, the words of Judas."

That caused a little stir.

When they built the cathedral in San Francisco a long time ago, maybe 40 years ago, there was similar criticism. But Dorothy Day said, "This belongs to everybody – the poor – everybody. And the poor deserve nice things and works of art."

She defended it.

Cardinal Roger Mahoney in Los Angeles was criticized for the $170 million spent on the cathedral that was just finished – a huge complex.

About a year and a half ago, I was with him at dinner. I was out there to speak in his archdiocese, and we were alone and got talking. I asked him about that cathedral.

He said, "You know, I got that money myself, from people. A whole lot of it was from Jewish people. They said, "People can't come to our synagogue, but everybody can go to your cathedral, and the city would be different without your cathedral. People will come from all over and enjoy this art."

Right down the street from St. Mary's Medical Center at St. Joseph Parish in Saginaw, the people built a $2.5 million church. Somebody could say, "Who do they think they are?"

Well, they are people who believe that money is well spent.

St. Mary's Medical Center in Saginaw; April 14, 2003; Jn 12:1-11.

Wealth and investments

I was recently in Turkey, visiting some of the sites where St. Paul visited.

Turkish currency is not based on the dollar. It's based on lire. I have here in my hand a one million lire note. In fact, I've got two of them.

Two million lire! I'm rich!

The truth is, one million Turkish lire . . . is worth about 16 cents.

Something struck me when I changed some money and received my first one million lire note. I thought, "At the end of time, a million dollars in U.S. currency won't even be worth as much as this one million lire note.

"All the money I have will be worthless.

"Any prestige I might have had will be worthless.

"Whatever car I had will be worthless.

"Whatever clothes I had will be worthless."

Somehow, simply holding a one million lire note in my hand made me experience this truth in a new way.

Advent is a time when we try to get a perspective by looking to the past, the present and the future. In that perspective, we ask ourselves, "What do I want to invest in?"

I don't need an investment counselor to do that. Jesus gives us the answer: Invest your life, your possessions, everything you have . . . invest it in the reign of God.

First Sunday of Advent/B cycle; 1 Cor 1:3-9; December 1, 2002.

Part VII
On gratitude, lessons, and pearls . . .

On gratitude, lessons, and pearls . . .

—ɯ—

Ken Untener didn't wear a bishop's ring or a pectoral cross. He chose to live on the salary of a diocesan priest.

When he traveled to the Vatican for his ad *limina* visits with the pope, he had to borrow formal bishop's attire from bishop friends. He rarely used the official title Bishop (much less *Very Reverend, Your Excellency or Your Grace*). To family and close friends, he was Kenny. When new employees addressed him as "Bishop," he'd quickly correct them, "You can call me Ken."

He described his average day as "preaching and meeting with people, ministering to the basic truths of our faith – very 'normal' activities." He was known for his quick wit and sense of humor, his piano playing and his cigar. One time in the seminary, he was asked at the last minute to play the organ for a special Mass. Caught unprepared, he took the then-popular theme from the Debbie Reynolds movie "Tammy," slowed it down and played it reverently as the faithful entered the seminary chapel.

Around the Saginaw diocesan offices, he'd stop by unexpectedly to chat with staff. He knew their families, baptized their children, and officiated at their weddings. He organized an annual cherry-spitting contest and Christmas door decorating contest (which he always won, once by stealing a staff person's lavishly decorated door and installing it at his own office). At diocesan Christmas parties, he'd whip up his infamous Glugg drink, which he gleefully ladled out to the unsuspecting.

He could be fiercely competitive – whether it was the weekly Sunday *New York Times* crossword puzzle or a friendly game of poker, or pick-up hockey. Despite his extroverted nature in crowds, he was also an introvert who said he could see himself living in a monastery. In the early morning's quiet, he'd settle in his easy chair with a cup of coffee, pipe in hand, deep in thought and prayer in a small room off his office at the Diocesan Center. Friends and journalists described Ken as soft-spoken, inspirational, down-to-earth, visionary. He was careful to never criticize Church teachings, but he believed even controversial issues needed to be talked about.

"The problem with being a bishop is there are no lateral moves," he explained. "You can only go up. That stops many bishops from being alive to the moment because they worry it might cost them a promotion to archbishop. They wait to say what they think with the idea that it'll be easier when they are an archbishop. Then when they become an archbishop, they think they may become a cardinal. And then you get to be a cardinal and you think, maybe I'll become pope. So you end up always looking ahead and not taking a chance on saying what you really think."

Bishop Francis Reh had been pleased to learn Ken would succeed him as Saginaw's next bishop. Like Cardinal Dearden, Bishop Reh had attended the Second Vatican Council, and he brought its vision to the Saginaw Diocese – a direction that Ken continued and expanded. Ken loved the Church. He wanted people to want to come to Mass and to be enriched by it, and he looked hard and long at how the liturgy was celebrated. He constantly thought up new and different ways to engage people in the Church. Staff frequently received a phone call from him while he was on the road: "I was just driving and I happened to think . . ."

His sale of the bishop's mansion, the hockey-playing, and his charismatic personality made him a media favorite – locally and internationally. He was the one-legged bishop who lives in his car and plays hockey, his priest friends would joke. And Ken, who had wanted to be a writer, respected the media. When he had been in the Detroit Archdiocese, he had hosted a weekly ecumenical television show, written editorials for the diocesan newspaper, and even served a stint as diocesan spokesman. He wrote a book on liturgy, penned articles for the Catholic and secular press, and recorded videotapes.

In 1995, Ken surprised Saginaw by announcing he would take a four-month sabbatical in 1997 to read, write, and pray. He decided to drive to Menlo Park, California, to be near St. Patrick Seminary and its theological library. He would live at the residence of his friend, John Quinn, the retired archbishop of San Francisco.

Ken returned to Saginaw with a new resolve to cut back on his out-of-town speaking engagements, to do more writing, and to prepare the diocese for a future with fewer priests.

In 2000, in an effort to encourage diocesan parishioners to return to Lent's traditional practices, he introduced a six-minute Lenten book of reflection, called the *Little Black Book*. More than 125,000 copies were distributed that first year. Realizing he was on to something, the next year he expanded *Little Books* to include books for the Advent and Easter seasons, and later for stewardship. Today, more than three million *Little Books* are distributed worldwide and are available in several languages. The whole purpose of *Little Books*, as Ken put it, was simply "to help people to pray."

While on sabbatical, Ken had finished his second book, "Preaching Better," which was published in 1999. Ever since he had begun teaching homiletics at St. John's Seminary back in the 1970s, he had informally polled people about what they liked and didn't like about homilies. In 1993, he had set up a homily group program in Saginaw where he and a group of six preachers would meet with a theologian and a journalist for four weeks to critique their homilies. His book was based on what he learned from the polls and the homily groups.

One of people's biggest complaints was that preachers tried to fit too many ideas and thoughts into their homilies. Homilists, he found, needed "to focus on just one core thought and stay with it. I refer to it as a 'pearl' that I describe as a core thought with depth, a valuable insight to be treasured."

Source of it all

---

*T*his morning it was cold in my room when I got up at the crack of dawn.

I turned on the nice, hot shower, and it would have been really good if I had thought to say, "God, thanks for the hot water."

The things that we have around us all the time – we realize that these are good, but the connection we need to make is that the source of it all (really, no matter how hard you work for it, even if you built the house yourself and put in the hot water tank) – the source of it all is God.

I nudge myself to think of more things that in the course of an ordinary day I can say thank you for, realizing that the source of all of the good things is God. Besides thanking God for the fruits of the earth and for the stars in the sky, to thank God for the hot water, for the Red Wings winning the Stanley Cup . . . for the little things . . . for big things . . . the stuff all around us.

"Thank you" is beautiful in every language. It comes to our lips easily. It's our most beautiful prayer. It's Eucharist. It's the best thing we can do, the easiest possible way to pray.

If I could just tune my mind into that, I would pray the music of that word many, many times, every day of my life.

Thanksgiving; Lk 19:41-44; St. Boniface Parish, Bay City; November 23, 1995.

First things first

I'm going to tell you a secret about me.

For some years now, the first words I say every morning after I get up (well, not always the *first* words. Sometimes the first words are, "Oh, it's raining again!") – so it's not always the *first* words that I say, but it's what I say as soon as I start brushing my teeth, for by that time I have to look at myself in the mirror. I memorized something from Scripture in the Old Testament, and this is what I say: "Unless the Lord builds the house, in vain do the builders labor."

And then I promise myself that I won't go back to bed.

What do you think that means? Why would the people who wrote the Psalms write that? *Unless the Lord builds the house, in vain do the builders labor.*

Unless we're doing what God has called us to do, it will never work. It's true what Jesus said: "It's the Father who does everything in me." He wasn't faking when he said that. He was trying to teach us something.

It's God who does great things through me. I don't care whether you're a little child or an old grandpa or grandma. Every day God wants to do great things through us. They might not seem great; they won't get in the paper, but God sends us every day to do wonderful things. God is acting in us, and we can do the most marvelous thing, and know that it is God who helps us do it.

But if I decide (that's why I have to tell myself this every day) that I know what's right and I'm going to do this and the heck with God – then I'm not going to do what God wants me to do that day.

Maybe God wants me to spend some time with little kids instead of doing some big, important stuff.

Maybe God wants me to visit somebody in the hospital when I don't think I have time to do that.

But if that's what God wants me to do, well, unless the Lord's building the house, there's no sense in trying to build one because it really will never work.

Religious education at St. John the Evangelist Parish, Essexville; Jn 6:22-39; April 15, 1991.

If I were raising children

I'd be the last person to write a book about how to raise children, but when I see what parents do, I stand back in wonder and awe.

But if I were raising children, there is one thing I know I would do. I would make sure that my children felt, experienced, and were tuned in to the presence of God all around them, for it is God who brings about the greatness I would want for my children.

In my home, there would be good religious symbols. We would thank God together before our meals. That's the kind of air I would want them to breathe.

I'd make sure that my children learned how to pray, not just grace before meals, but I'd want them to know our rich traditions of prayer. I'd want them to know how to pray just as much as I'd want them to know how to walk and how to read.

I'd want to make sure they had a good family life, including the family life of a parish where they would connect with other people who believe . . . ordinary people who believe and try to live these extraordinary truths.

I'd want to make sure they learned the Word of God. Jesus told a parable where the seed sown was the Word, and it produced one hundredfold. Then there was the time the woman in the crowd called out to Jesus, "Blest is the womb that bore you and the breasts that nursed you." And he said, "Rather, blest are those who hear the Word of God and keep it."

Finally, I'd want to make sure that they gathered around the holy table at Mass. It is here on the altar where they place the little pieces of their life, symbolized by the bread and wine, and entrust them to God who gives them meaning and greatness. And it is here where they are fed with the Bread of Life.

All these apparently little things are the things I would, most of all, be sure my children had.

Eleventh Sunday in Ordinary Time; Mk 4:26-34/B cycle; 100th anniversary of St. Columbkille Parish in Sheridan Corners; June 15, 1997.

It's always now

---

*A*t the end of his Gospel, Matthew sets us thinking about getting ready and being prepared and staying awake and taking action, not missing opportunities.

It got me thinking about opportunities missed and opportunities taken in my life, about deadlines missed and deadlines fulfilled, and about hourglasses and time.

One of the things that I tell myself, a principle of life that I have formulated in my old age (I'm 58 years old), this I know, this you can take to the bank, this is true: There's never a good time to do something difficult.

For example, there's never a good time to start a diet because there's a holiday coming or a birthday coming or a party coming.

There's never a good time to face up to those who have to be faced up to because it's going to be the weekend, or it's going to be Christmas. You don't want to wreck their Christmas.

There's never a good time to do something difficult.

The mistake that I make is to picture the hourglass of my life as very, very full, with all the sand in it – it's going to take years to run out, so I can wait.

Well, I've learned that with God, it's always now.

I've learned in my own life, and by 33 years of being a priest and watching the lives of others, that God uses smaller timers and time-pieces in calling us to change, and that I need to be ready and listen. Tune in. I've learned that there's never a good time to do something difficult.

With God, the time is always now. God is as present to me as God is ever going to be. God's grace is as full for me as it ever will be.

First Sunday of Advent/A cycle; Mt 24:37-44; Mass at St. Frances X. Cabrini Parish in Vassar and St. Bernard Parish in Millington; December 3, 1995.

Editor of the parables

I could have helped Jesus edit his parables, and I think I could have improved them.

For example, the parable of the prodigal son. Jesus had a terrific story there, but he should have edited out the last scene. He ended with the father and the son reunited – everybody's happy. Why bring up the older brother who gets mad? Just end it there, everybody's happy.

Or the parable about the workers receiving the same payment, regardless of how many hours they worked. A simple editing job would do the trick. All you've got to do is reverse the order of payment. Bring on stage the people who were hired at dawn and they get their pay. They're happy and they go offstage. Then, when the last ones get there, they're happy and everybody goes home happy because nobody knows what anybody else got.

But the whole point of these two parables is the lavish generosity of God. It addresses those of us who sometimes think that in God's generosity and mercy, he ought to pay more attention to human work and struggle and merit.

I suppose that the feelings portrayed by the grumblers in the parable about the workers would be something like people in our country could feel when new immigrants come in today. We've worked long and hard to build up this country, fought wars to defend it, built up an economy, and here they come and they just take advantage of all these things that we have worked long and hard to build up.

You might say about this parable that you could never run a business that way, and that's true. But this parable is not about running a business. This parable is about the kingdom of God. This parable is about what a Church is meant to be. This parable is about what a parish is meant to be, because a parish is not a business.

Oh, there are business aspects about a parish – you have to pay the bills, you have to keep it up, you have to hire personnel. But a parish is the strangest kind of place. You'd never run a business this way. We take in sinners. We don't get just the clean, the elite. Come on in, all of us, sinners. And when people don't live up to their commitments to the parish . . . come on in, anyway. Come, receive the sacraments. Hear the word. When people come late, leave early, don't sing . . . we say, come on in.

A parish is a strange place. It's the only place in the world where it's not run like the strict rules of a business or other organization . . . It operates on the principle that a parish is something you never have to earn. God's mercy does it. You don't earn it. We don't try to make all the distinction. You come gather around the table.

Don't be too quick to think that it's easier for a priest or a bishop or a cardinal to be holy. Don't be too quick to think that it's easier to pray . . . that it's easier to love your neighbor . . . that it's easier to have a deep-down faith, hope, and love. The Gospel teaches us not to try to sort it out.

Which is harder: To get hired at dawn and work all day in the heat of the sun, or to stand in the marketplace and be passed over all day? I don't know. It's probably about even, which is the way the landowner paid off.

Which is easier: To be a cardinal of the Church or to be a Catholic in the pew, maybe the back pew? I don't know. Often it probably comes out about even, which is the way the landowner paid off.

Which is harder: To be married and raise a family, or to be single, or to be separated, or widowed, or to be celibate for the kingdom of God? Which is harder? I don't know. It probably comes out about even, which is the way the landowner paid off.

It's hard for everyone to be a disciple. We can't sort out for whom it's easy or for whom it's hard, because it's hard for everybody. We just try not to make the distinctions which Jesus says not to make, and simply come together.

Twenty-fifth Sunday in Ordinary Time/A cycle; Mt 20:1-16; 125th anniversary of St. Brigid of Kildare Parish in Midland; September 22, 1996.

Simple advice

When I was teaching preaching at St. John's Seminary, I was trying to put together an evaluation of what makes a good homily.

It got very complex – about two pages. The beginning, the ending, articulation, the examples – all the things you would check in evaluating a homily.

I used to send those evaluation forms out to people who would listen to my students' homilies. They would check all these questions on the forms, and the last question was always: "On the whole, what did you think of the homily?"

Very often they would check, very good, very good, very good, very good . . . articulations, examples . . . "On the whole, what did you think of the homily?" Not good.

So I eventually found myself making it all very simple. I used to tell my students that to give a good homily, say something that the people will remember, and the memory will help them live their lives.

That was my simple statement.

Do the people remember and does the remembering help them live their lives?

Thirty-first Sunday in Ordinary Time/B cycle; Mk 12:28-32.

Tell the truth

---

7 remember one time at St. John's Seminary when I gave the homily for a special Mass that included bishops and many others.

Afterwards, I found out that just about every group there thought that I had pointed the homily at them. A couple of bishops thought I was speaking particularly to them. Some of the faculty thought I was talking to them. Then I found out that quite a number of students thought that the homily was aimed at them.

I thought to myself, "I must have hit upon something pretty good here to have struck such a chord in so many different people."

The truth is, I didn't have any of them in mind.

As usual, I was preaching to myself. I had been asked to give the homily on fairly short notice, and I simply tried to preach what the Scriptures spoke to me.

As Mark Twain once said, "When in doubt, tell the truth."

Chrism Mass; April 4, 1992.

Trade secret

I'm going to tell you a trade secret.
When I have a major talk to write and the pressure is on, I learned a long time ago to think small. I try to craft a jewel rather than build a garage. When I do that, I think deep thoughts, and when I do that, I tend to leave more room for God.

There's something to be said for thinking small.

To plant the seed of greatness, think small . . . the tiny seed.

Baccalaureate at All Saints High School, Bay City; Mk 4:30-36; June 4, 1997.

Deep in the heart

Strange as it may seem, when it comes to talking about our relationship to God, it's hardest for us to tell "the secrets of our heart" to those we know well.

You'd think it would be just the opposite. But it isn't.

Fly me to Chicago, put me in front of a large crowd, and I can speak easily and honestly and with passion about my faith.

But put me together with "my own" and it's not so easy. For some reason, it's not easy to tell "our own" the secrets of our heart – the secrets of our closeness to God . . . a closeness that is so simple, so intimate, so personal, that we're afraid it might seem silly, even childish.

I wonder if we don't all fear that our relationship with God is so particular that it won't be understood by someone else. We avoid speaking of the profound within us because it seems so simple. That's a big mistake because the deeper it gets, the simpler it gets. I think we prefer to speak "correctly" rather than cutting to the bone. I think we prefer to talk about doctrine.

The truth is, I'd really like to know what God is like to someone else.

A fellow wrote to me and said that one day he was struck by something in one of our *Little Books*. Because he knew his wife read the same thing that day, he asked her what she thought of it. They ended up talking – really talking – about God. He said it was the first time the two of them had ever talked together about their faith. They had talked about Church teachings and Church issues, but never about who God was to them.

What about close friends, or not-so-close but trusted acquaintances? Or co-workers? Do we do that with them? I'm not sure we do.

I'm not talking about getting preachy.

I'm not talking about turning every barbeque into a Bible study.

I'm not talking about shifting into a "pulpit tone" and always bringing "God-talk" into regular conversation (when you have to shift gears to talk about God, "it ain't real").

I'm talking about doing it naturally, not superficially or artificially.

I'm talking about doing it because God truly is the normal back-drop of my life, always there. I'm talking about doing it naturally because God really is consciously part of my deep-down self.

There are times for it, and there are places for it. I wonder how often it happens? I wonder if it happens often enough?

I do know that it often happens at death – not every death, but the death of someone we love.

I did it with my mother when I was alone with her, and she was dying. But to tell the truth, I wasn't sure if she could hear me, and perhaps that helped me do it.

I do know I spoke to her the secrets of my heart, about her God and my God, and I think it was the first time.

Chrism Mass; March 26, 2002.

Tony's Shop

I remember in the early days when I was getting my wooden leg
fitted and adjusted for the first time.

There was an old shop on Woodward Avenue in Detroit where I
went. Tony (the owner) had lost both his legs in a railroad accident.
He was an Italian fellow who simply learned the trade himself and
built up his own business.

Back in those days, it wasn't a very big shop and when you were
there, you simply sat around in this big room where they did all the
work. There would be six or seven people sitting there getting adjustments or something, and the workers would be performing their craft.
You were always there for hours on end.

It was something to be in that room. There was a lot of activity
and sawdust in the air, and it was very, very informal. Now they have
built a new shop. It is big and modern, and they have separate rooms
for everyone.

I was talking to Tony a while back and he said that it was better the
old way.

I asked him why.

He said it was better because a lot happened in that room to the
people who had lost a leg or two legs or an arm. They were there together and just being together and talking to one another was a tremendous means of support. The people didn't feel sorry for themselves.
They couldn't because there they were with others who were in the
same boat. It accomplished far more than all the individual counseling
that a person might receive when they go through a trauma like that.

Well, we need to make sure we do that in our churches. Sometimes
our churches are built more like Tony's *new* shop with people isolated
from one another.

But there is something about being together with the wood chips
and the sawdust and one another, and sort of being thrown together

that way, and understanding one another and being close and conversing and, well, just being together.

We should be trying to build our churches that way and they ought to *be* that way because that's what churches are – gathering places for people with handicaps.

Seventeenth Sunday in Ordinary Time/C cycle; Lk 11:1-13.

Shroud of Turin

$\mathcal{E}$arly this morning as I was driving in from Sandusky [Michigan], I turned the news on and I heard that the long-awaited report on the Shroud of Turin had been released.

They had been working on this for a couple of years, using the highest scientific data. They were trying to determine whether or not this shroud really dated from the first century and could be (as was long believed) the true image of Jesus Christ.

The conclusive scientific evidence is that it is no more than 700 years old, and that it is a portrait of Jesus, not the shroud that covered him when he was buried.

Now that did not come as any surprise for me. I never believed it was.

I have read some of the reports about the shroud and some of its history. It really didn't have any historical record until about the 13th or 14th century. Bishops (back then when it was being displayed) were very cool about the shroud, and did not endorse it (and I always believe whatever a bishop says).

But as the centuries went on (as happens), it gained more and more credibility, and many people believed that this was truly the shroud in which Jesus was buried.

Now I suppose there are some people whose faith is shaken by this release today, and it's too bad. It's too bad when we wrap ourselves in things that are more or less on the margin or on the periphery of our central belief. There sometimes is an inclination to do that, to become (to use a pun) all wrapped up in the shroud as the basis of our faith and devotion.

But the heart of our faith is the life and the death and the rising of Jesus. The substance of our lives as Christians is to believe as he taught that we are children of God. We are meant to look like and to act like this God who forgives, who reaches out to the poor, who is loving, who is gentle, who is a peacemaker, who always brings life, not death, who dreams great dreams, who lives a life that can never die.

Sometimes, devotional memorabilia can be ways of avoiding the hard realities of living up to our faith. They can distract us or give us the illusion that we can have shortcuts to heaven, instead of just living out the core of our faith.

Physicians' Gathering; October 13, 1988.

Why I memorize the Gospels

---

*F*or about 20 years now, I've had the practice of memorizing the Gospel for each Eucharist. I do it because of the effect it has on me.

You see, Gospel passages are like miniature paintings. We don't catch the beauty of them with simply a glance. We need to look closely, take our time with them, catch the tiny details, the artistic structure.

There are many ways to do that. My way is to memorize them.

I don't have a photographic memory. I have to work hard, but I figure if youngsters can memorize commercials, I can memorize Gospels. I make sure to do it word for word because the Gospels are precious texts. But it will sound different and you might think that I am paraphrasing or modernizing the language.

I am not.

They sound different because the Gospel passages were stories told over and over again for 40, 50 years before they were written. And when they are told as a story, they come alive in their original form.

Raising of Lazarus; Jn 11:1-45.

Driving down I-75

———————

I was driving down I-75 thinking about conversion.

What kind of conversion is involved for those preparing for the Easter sacraments? What kind of conversion are all of us called to during Lent?

Is it a conversion from a life of debauchery and crime and paganism and atheism? For some people, that certainly is not true.

Is it simply a conversion from one Christian Church to another, from being a Lutheran or a Methodist or a Presbyterian to becoming a Catholic? No. That is not a great conversion. That is a small bridge to cross in these days when the Christian Churches have moved closer to unity.

Then what kind of conversion is this?

It is the same conversion preached by Jesus. It is a conversion from the basic teachings of the Old Testament to the teachings of the Gospel. It is a decision to take seriously and live the teachings of Jesus.

As I was driving, an image came to mind. Sometimes you see a road running alongside the expressway, and it goes in the same direction for awhile, but then the road goes off somewhere else, and you can't see it anymore.

Roads like that are different from the expressway. They are not as wide or as straight. You can have a hard time getting around slow-moving trucks. The roads twist and turn through the countryside, and then through towns. It's a hard, longer drive.

Traveling along as part of the culture is like traveling on the expressway.

Deciding to live the Gospel is like traveling the side roads.

Traveling on the expressway is like tuning in to the best of our country's values and way of life. You think it goes in the same direction as those other roads, and that you are following the Gospel.

Wrong.

To live the Gospel, you have to get off that expressway and get on the road that runs alongside it. You have to leave the "good and normal" way to travel the more difficult road. You have to put up with traffic and detours, and go through towns that aren't as "antiseptic" as turnpike service plazas. You will see more poor people, some junkyards, and many things you might have missed.

To follow the way of the Gospel, you have to get off the expressway.

Too many Christians are sailing along on the expressway. We bishops and priests have often been on the expressway. Religious have sometimes been there, and lay people, good upstanding Catholics, are often there, too.

We've let ourselves believe that we can sail along on the expressway of our culture and know that we are following the way of the Lord.

We have fooled ourselves.

Rite of Election; February 17, 1991.

Moment of prayer

$\mathcal{A}$t the first Mass this morning, when Fr. John Mullet was the celebrant, I was able to sit down during Communion and think and pray and watch.

I don't often get to sit there and just enjoy praying. Usually I'm doing what's going on.

I sat there and it was a graced moment (God does these things to us sometimes). I just sat there and watched people coming forward to communion, and it really was a moment of prayer – the kind that you can't manufacture.

It just hit me and I soaked it all in, saying to myself, "They're just like me, and I'm just like them. We're all sinners and not perfect, but we're all good, too, trying to do our best."

I just imagined what the story must be behind each face. But in those moments I had a sense of the goodness behind each face. After all, these were people who had come to be with the Lord, who had come to ask the Lord for help to make it through the week.

They had come to put their lives on the altar, represented by those gifts brought forward. They put it all in the hands of the Lord – the ordinary stuff of life that is precious in the hands of the Lord. There's a goodness, a pearl of great price, in the soil of our lives.

It was a great moment as I sat there and took that in, in a way that I hadn't felt before. It was God's grace, a moment of prayer.

Seventeenth Sunday in Ordinary Time/A cycle; Mt.13:44-46; installation of Fr. John Mullet at St. Philip Neri Parish in Coleman and St. Anne Parish in Edenville; July 28, 1996.

Death of the Church?

Some months ago, I was giving a talk to a fairly small group. During the question period, a person brought up the sex-abuse scandal and said, quite sincerely and quite fearfully, "Is this going to be the end of the Catholic Church?"

I responded that this crisis is something we have to take very seriously – and humbly – and we have to face it squarely. But the Church isn't going to fall apart.

At times like this, it can be helpful to scan the life story of the Church and see some of the problems it has gone through.

In the early centuries, there were terrible persecutions. Some Christians, rather than face death, gave in and renounced their faith. But that's not all. They not only *gave in,* but *turned in* friends and family members who were then tortured and killed. This caused terrible, terrible anger. When the persecution was over and these informers wanted to return to the Church, the Church had to deal with split families, split communities. They had an awful time.

Toward the end of the first millennium, many, many priests were untrained, uneducated, even illiterate. There was no system in place to train them.

About 1,000 years ago, the Church broke in half – a split, a divorce between the Eastern and Western Church, and we were left breathing on one lung. (Although there has been some healing, much of the Eastern Church is still separate today.)

In the late Middle Ages, by political maneuvering and intrigue, Italian noble families (Borgias, Medicis) one after the other got their sons elected pope. The main interest of some of these popes was power, money, pleasure. This was a very bad stretch of our history. At times, there were two different popes, both claiming the throne of Peter. Once there were even three popes.

Then in the 17th and 18th centuries, there came what was called the "enlightenment." A wave of new discoveries in science caused many to think that we no longer needed to believe in God. Reason had replaced faith, and everything could be explained scientifically. Those who believed in God were simply fools clinging to false legends. Many began to ask (as I had been asked a short while back), "Is this the end of the Church?"

So, I told this brief life story of the Church to the person who asked the question. I explained that if it proves anything at all, it proves that we shouldn't place our ultimate hope in the abilities of popes or bishops, or in a good public-relations department.

Our hope rests on the unbreakable bond of the Spirit, which Christ sent upon us . . . a Spirit who is with us for better or for worse, for richer or for poorer, in sickness and in health, until the end of time.

Feast of SS. Peter and Paul.

Part VIII
The last word . . .

The last word . . .

—⁓—

"I don't pray to avoid sickness and death. I pray that I will be able to live well and, then, to die well."
— Ken Untener

On February 13, 2004, the Diocese of Saginaw released a press statement that Ken Untener had been diagnosed with a bone marrow disorder called myelodysplastic syndrome.

He hadn't been feeling well in the weeks before Christmas, but presumed he had the flu. When his health didn't improve after the New Year, his doctors ordered more tests and found that he was critically low on blood and at risk of major infection. He went quickly to Barbara Ann Karmanos Cancer Institute in downtown Detroit, and a sample of his bone marrow was sent to California for analysis.

"Interesting how something like this so affects one's prayer," Ken wrote to his priests and pastoral administrators in telling them of his medical condition. "God has no difficulty getting my attention. I count on your prayers, too."

After several weeks at Karmanos, his doctors told Ken that chemotherapy was not working. Besides his bone marrow disorder, he was also suffering from acute leukemia. He might as well prepare to die.

"My bone marrow problem is a serious one," he wrote to his staff, clergy, and religious. "But in my mind I can picture myself looking at the people in your assembly right now, and one person after another could stand up and talk about a serious health problem in your family.

"We're all in this together, facing life and death, personal successes and personal failures, sin and grace. At every Eucharist I very consciously stand with you as together we all stand with Christ in his great continuing act of giving us entirely to the Father, and letting us join with him in doing that, knowing that in the Father's hands it all ultimately leads to life. . . . We *are* in this together."

After his release from the hospital, he decided to rest on the familiar grounds of St. John's Provincial Seminary, where he had once been rector. When he began to need more medical care, he was moved to the infirmary of the IHM Motherhouse in Monroe. His oldest sister was a member of the Sisters, Servants of the Immaculate Heart of Mary and was living there. It was also where his mother had spent her last days.

Ken had always planned to work until he was 75, the mandatory age when all bishops must submit their resignation to the pope. When the media would speculate that he might be named bishop of another diocese, he'd laugh it off and tell them he wasn't going anywhere. His will even stipulated that he would be buried in Saginaw.

After he got sick, Ken never had a chance to say goodbye to his priests and staff in Saginaw. He didn't expect to die outside of Saginaw. When family talked to him the night before he died, he reminded them, "It ain't over yet."

Ken Untener died on Saturday, March 27, 2004. He was 66 years old.

His body was returned to Saginaw at last for his funeral Mass and burial.

Things that last

I just turned 60 this past August.

I don't know at what age it begins to happen, but you look back on your life a little differently. You notice things that last and things that pass.

We realize that some things will be gone and some things will continue by looking at the brief history of our own lives.

For example, the house that I grew up in is gone. It's leveled (I was sure they would make a shrine out of it!). It's gone. I have the memories but the house itself did not last.

Some things pass and some things last. . . . The old piano that we had is gone, too, but my love for music and the music that's in me continues.

Some things last. . . . My education. I was educated well by sisters who taught me in a Catholic school from the first grade to the 12th grade. I had a classical education, and it lasts. It will always be with me.

Some relationships didn't last. There were high school friends or other friends along the way. Some friendships last and will be a part of me in the reign of God.

My relationship with God, which my parents taught me (it was the air we breathed), well, that lasts forever.

When you have that perspective, you begin to invest your heart in things that last, and not too heavily in things that pass.

First Sunday of Advent/C cycle; Lk 21:25-28, 34-38; St. Mary Parish, Albee; November 29-30, 1997.

Happy to be ordained

I am happy to be a member of the Roman Catholic Church. I would divide my life into a period before 1969 and another period after 1969. That year I was sent to Rome for graduate studies.

My formation had been the same as the formation of many priests. I was brought up with the catechism. I was brought up on the Tridentine Mass. I went to a seminary that was more like a monastery. My early years of priesthood were still in the trajectory that might be called the pre-Vatican II Church.

Then when I had the gift of those two years in Rome, I had time to read and think. Also, as the Church moved along, I became caught up in that. There began the second part of my life – at least so far.

But I have never felt a rending between those two. In the Old Testament story of Naboth and his vineyard, the reason why he didn't want to give up that vineyard is because it wasn't just a field to him. It was his whole heritage. That land that had been given to him by his ancestors was more than a field . . . it was his heritage.

I'm grateful that I've never had to give up my heritage. I have never felt – ever – a rending between the Church before 1969 and after.

I was taught the Sermon on the Mount in grade school.

I was taught to love the poor.

I was taught: Blessed are the peacemakers.

I was taught to love God, love your neighbor.

I was taught the Prologue of John's Gospel.

I was taught the same heritage that sustains me today.

In one of Pope John Paul II's encyclicals, he touches on that very point: "Continuity and renewal are a proof of the perennial value of the Church's teachings."

Continuity and renewal.

He says, "This two-fold dimension is typical of her teaching, especially in the social sphere. That's perhaps the clearest example. On the one hand, it is constant for it remains identical to its fundamental inspiration. On the other hand, it is ever new because it is subject to the necessary and opportune adaptations suggested by the changes in historical conditions and by the unceasing flow of the events which are the setting of the lives of people in society."

Continuity and renewal.

I am grateful that I have been able (just like Naboth) to cling to my heritage because I'm happy with this heritage. This is a Church that I love.

I am also happy to be an ordained priest. As I look back and as I think about it today, there's always been a certain clarity to the call that I have experienced. It has never been, for me, a fuzzy call to be a Roman Catholic ordained priest. I think it's because it has been clear to me that it is a commitment to a person and not to a job description.

For me, it has been a certain kind of relationship to the Lord and to his body, the Church. And it always seemed to me that this was where I was meant to be.

Now, there's been lots of confusion about different things along the way, and I've always felt a little bit like Simon of Cyrene. He knew that he was where he ought to be in relationship to Jesus – however many feet he was behind him. Simon didn't always know where he was going. He didn't always know why or how he got there, but it seemed right to be there.

I've not always understood what a priest should be doing today, and I know that things have changed since 1963 when I was ordained. But I have never doubted that this special relationship – and each disciple has a different relationship and not everybody carried that cross behind Jesus in the same way as Simon – that the relationship of mine to this body, the Church, was where I ought to be. It was always perfectly clear.

It was to be a public relationship.

It was to be in leadership.

It was to proclaim God's word, to celebrate, and to do it for life.

For that clarity, I am very grateful. And for this priesthood, I am very happy.

I am happy, as I look back, to be a parish priest.

There are many kinds of priests that you can be, and there are many roles of leadership in the Church.

I think I have something of the monk in me (monk, not monkey). At one time, I thought I might want to be a Trappist. I like solitude and there are times when that side of me comes through.

But it has seemed to me that the Gospel never comes closer to life than it does in a parish, and I have been happy to be there. All of my priesthood has been lived in a parish, except those two years when I studied in Rome, and then when I was rector for three years of St. John's Provincial Seminary (although even then I went out every weekend to the same parish).

I am happy to be at that place where the Gospel is tested most and expressed more richly to me . . . in a parish. In a parish, the history of the Church that has never been written happens, the history of the Church that happens in the day-in and day-out lives of people, and probably a history that can't be written and we'll know only in the kingdom. But, in a parish, I've seen it in its unfolding.

I'm happy to be a parish priest. Lastly, a parish priest of the Church of Saginaw.

As I look back on these 25 years, one of the things I have observed is that the Lord has connected me with people who were good for me.

I mean that very much.

As I look back, there are people that I didn't search out, with whom my life became somehow connected, and it was very, very good for me. God has connected me those people in Saginaw. As Joe Imesch [bishop of Joliet, Illinois] can testify (because I say this outside this diocese), this is an unusual group of people. But with this group of people, with this presbyterate – this is an awfully good place to be.

I was just down to Detroit for the closing of St. John's Seminary, and I realized that I'm not part of that anymore. I didn't know where some of the guys were assigned. I realized that this has long since passed me by, and that I am a member of the presbyterate of the Church of Saginaw.

Once again, God has connected me with people who were good for me.

Saginaw diocesan priests' jubilee; June 13, 1988.

Why I stay in the Church

Why am I staying in the Church?

Because there is so much in this community and its history that I can affirm, so much in this community from which, like so many others, I draw life.

I am staying in the Church because, along with the other members of this community of faith, we are the Church. (One should not confuse the Church with its apparatus or administrators; nor leave it to them alone to mold the community.)

I am staying in the Church because, even with all the strong objections made against it, here I am at home. Here all the great questions are asked: The where and whence, and why and how of humanity and this world.

I could not think of turning my back on the Church any more than, in the political sphere, I could turn my back on democracy which, in its own way no less than the Church, is being misused and abused.

Everything that blossoms, dies

---

7 like summer.

I like blue skies and sunshine, and I like to play golf a whole lot. Probably because of golf, I like the summer best.

Now I don't know if this simply happens because you get older, but I think summer has been going by more quickly this year than any other. I remember thinking about that a while back. I was wishing that there were some way that I could slow summer down and hang onto it. It seemed as though it had just gotten here and by then it was half over. I wanted summer to stay.

The last time I felt like that was when I was a youngster going to school. Along about mid-August, I would notice that the sisters had come back to the convent from the motherhouse. It was an omen that school was about to begin. I felt terrible. The summer had seemed to go by so quickly.

Summer is a lot like life. Summer is a sign, a symbol of what happens in this life. I have come to believe that a key for understanding life and having a proper perspective on life is to know this: Everything that blossoms, dies.

That's not meant to be pessimistic. Blossoms are beautiful. We just simply have to realize that they pass along, just like summer. If we can treat things that way, we take them for what they are. We enjoy them rather than destroy them or destroy ourselves by trying to keep them. We do that, for example, when we try to take too many pictures and ruin the trip or the party or the wedding.

I remember as a youngster what I did when a couple of us got ice cream cones. I always wanted to see if I could make my ice cream cone last longer than my brothers and sisters. I wanted to finish last and let them watch me finish eating it.

But do you know what sometimes happened? I'd try to drag it out so long that the ice cream melted and I never got to enjoy it. "Whoever wishes to save his life will lose it, but whoever loses his life for my sake will find it . . ."

Everything that blossoms, dies. When we see things that way, we see them as they are. We live them and enjoy them, but never make the mistake of thinking we can hang onto them.

Whatever blossoms, dies. It is true of everything in life.

Sometimes children don't realize that. They don't want to grow up and leave home. Sometimes parents don't realize that. They don't want to let their children grow up and be on their own.

People want to hang onto their youth.

Athletes want to hang on to their careers.

Even good friendships can be passing, and we have to let them go.

It is true of our cars and our clothes and our bank accounts. They are all like summer.

To realize this is the beginning of wisdom. To forget this is to end up with an ice cream cone that is all melted and ruined.

Twenty-second Sunday in Ordinary Time/A cycle; Mt 16:21-27; Parent Rally, August 30, 1987.

A powerful faith

A friend of mine is a good theologian and good person. Her mother was dying of cancer, so she flew to where her mother lived and spent that last month with her.

Her mother was a good person, a well-read person. She had been a teacher and a good Catholic. Her mind was sharp to the end.

It was only a couple of days before she died, and she and my friend had several long conversations. Somehow or other, her mother made the comment, "You know, faith has always been my problem. It's always been tough."

My friend said, "Oh, mother, I am sure there are some tough things to believe, but I'm sure your faith is strong, solid, clear. You don't have to worry about it."

Her mother said, "Well, it's tough."

My friend said, "Well, okay, let's go through this. Let's check it out. Mother, do you believe in God?"

There was this pause, and my friend started to get worried a little bit. After all, this was going to be the easy question, you see. She was going to work up to some tougher ones in a minute.

Her mother said, "Yes, I do . . . but only if it's a God for everybody – the Hindus, the Buddhists. I don't want a narrow God."

My friend said, "That's good. Beneath it, that's what we believe. We don't always use the right words, but we do believe. Fine. We've always believed in that kind of God. Do you believe, Mother, in Jesus Christ?"

"Well, yeah, but I don't know if I like the words that you use sometimes. I think that sometimes it doesn't seem like he was even a human being. I believe he was absolutely unique and called by God. If you want to use Son of God for that, okay, but sometimes I don't like the way Jesus is talked about. But I believe in him and I believe what he taught."

"Good. Do you believe in life after death?"

Pause. "Yeah, I do. But sometimes I don't like the way that's described either. I just know that there is life. I don't know what it's like."

My friend said, "That's as far as I wanted to push it. I didn't ask any more."

Now some people might say, "Gee, her mother's faith was weak."

I want to say, "Gee, her faith was strong." That, on her deathbed, she could say that I really do believe in God, in Jesus, in life – that means so much more to me than somebody who just rattled off a whole list of things, afraid ever to look at them.

That's a powerful faith. That's a strong faith. That's faith on this side of the line.

Fourth Sunday in Ordinary Time/B cycle; Mk 1:21-28.

Story of the sparrow

I received a letter from a friend of mine who, in the course of the letter, wrote about something that struck me. She wrote:

"I can't remember what day – Monday, I think – I saw on my patio a scruffy little sparrow picking at the seeds that had fallen from the finch feeder. It was hurt, and could pick up seeds only slowly with the side of its beak. Its left leg and foot were hurt. It could hardly hop and would eat a few seeds and then rest.

"I thought it was near death. After picking so slowly at just a few seeds, it rested for an hour, maybe, in the sun, and then it flew low to the ground around the corner of the house."

She wrote about how it came back the next day and she began to watch for it.

"So I prayed for it whenever it came, and I prayed something to the effect that: 'God, it wouldn't lessen your worth or your concern for important things to be concerned also for this insignificant little hurt sparrow that is trying so hard to make it.'

"And sometimes when I prayed, I cried a little. By now, of course, I was attached and invested and watching for him, and I worried when it rained at night.

"All during the week he seemed to be getting stronger, still crippled though. Well, then it took a turn for the worse toward the end of the week. Saturday night, it stormed. Sunday, I felt sad, trying not to watch for him. He hadn't come by the time I left for Mass at 10:45. When I came back from Mass, I went to the patio door from habit and there he was, sitting up against the wall, eating.

"I was so happy. He looked good. Then two other sparrows came and, still crippled, he tried to hop when they hopped. And then they flew away and he flew with them. He hasn't been here since. I have a feeling he won't be back, but I think he'll make it.

"I'm telling you this because I trust you and I trust you won't laugh. I never asked that bird to come and all I did was provide for him so that God could do some healing. And it hasn't hurt God's reputation for doing important things to do a little thing like this, has it?"

Of course, it hasn't.

When I come before the Lord, and he brings up how there were little ones in my world – little creatures, relatives that were left out and hurt, poor people, people that deserve to be left out because of the way they act but shouldn't be – I'll say, "Well, you see, I've had a lot of other things to do."

God'll say, just like my friend's question, "It wouldn't have hurt your reputation for doing important things to have taken care of those little ones, would it?"

Twenty-fifth Sunday in Ordinary Time/B cycle; Mk 9:30-37; St. Vincent de Paul Parish in Bay City; September 17/18, 1988.

The storm

What do you think about when you see a storm, when there is a great wind and especially when there is thunder and lightning?

A lot of us think about God. People talk about God sending a lightning bolt to us. Somehow, lightning especially embodies God.

I got to thinking about that and I realize that this connecting of God with a storm has more to do with pagan mythology than with the God of Christianity.

In pagan mythology, there was a great battle between the gods and the forces of evil who were in the sea and in the storms and in the wind and the lightning and the thunder. In ancient mythology, the story of creation was really the story of the tug-of-war between the gods and the forces of the sea and water. The gods won out, and separated dry land from the waters.

The mythology is kind of in our bones, I think. I know if you have ever stood on a seashore at night and seen the dark sea and waves breaking – it is ominous. The few times that I have gone swimming at night, it's kind of frightening when you go into that dark water and you go underwater. You can't see anything, and the forces of evil somehow are symbolized by that water. The thunderstorms and the lightning – that seems to be God. Great power. Supernatural powers.

But look at the God revealed in the Scriptures and especially the full revelation of God in the person of Jesus Christ. It dawned on me that God is not the maker of the storms; he's the one who stops the storms. The kind of God that Jesus revealed is not a God who sends lightning bolts. He's not a God in dark clouds and great thunder.

He's a God who washes feet; a God who cries when a friend dies; a God who lays a gentle hand on sick people; a God who holds little children and blesses them; a God who, in the face of a storm that has his disciples frightened, calms the wind and the sea.

He's a God who stops the storms, not a God who makes the storms.

I remember one time as a youngster, there was a terrible thunderstorm at night. I guess my mother knew we were afraid. She got us together in the living room, and she got out a vigil light that we used now and then when we said the rosary.

She put the vigil light on the mantle, and we just sat there together to make sure that we were okay. The electricity was knocked out and that was the only light in the house.

I was thinking, looking back on that experience, that it wasn't the thunder and the lightning and the wind howling out there that symbolized God.

It was that little vigil light, the gentle flame that gave us light.

I hope everyone's image of God is the gentle one, and not the thunderstorm one.

Twelfth Sunday in Ordinary Time/B cycle; Mk 4:35-41.

In the hands of the Lord

I visited a woman in her mid-50s (I think) who was dying of cancer. Her family asked me to do this because they thought she was losing hope. She was at home and she was dying. She was skin-and-bones, and she couldn't talk. But she opened her eyes very wide and nodded her head when I asked if she knew who I was.

The family left me alone with her for a little bit. I told her that it has been my experience when I've been sick that it's the hardest time to pray.

Now you would think that when you are sick (especially when you are really sick and perhaps dying), you would pray the hardest and pray the best. But when you're in pain, it's hard even to think. It has been my experience that one of the hardest times to pray is when you are sick.

So I told her that. I told her that I didn't come with a lot of words. I didn't have answers as to why things like this happen, and I didn't have things to say that would make everything easier for her. And I knew she was having a hard time because her family knew that and told me.

I told her: The only thing I would suggest is that you try just to give this whole thing to the Lord, to put this whole thing in his hands, and just keep doing that over and over and over again. Life, death, suffering – those are things that are to be treated with great reverence, and not with easy answers and a lot of words. They belong in the hands of the Lord. In the hands of the Lord, these things come together and make sense and take on meaning.

She listened and I think it helped.

The Gospels tell us that if you have faith and if you trust, bad things may happen to you, but you don't have to be afraid of them because in the hands of the Lord, they can be life-giving. It doesn't mean that it will be easy – that woman died very soon after I visited. It doesn't mean we have simple answers.

It means that, in the hands of the Lord, dying can make sense and can produce life. In the hands of the Lord, things that are too much for us to understand and too much for us to handle take on meaning.

And it's enough.

Seventeenth Sunday in Ordinary Time/B cycle; Jn 6:1-15; St. Michael Parish in Port Austin and St. Joseph Parish in Argyle; July 23/24, 1988.

Minister, not the Messiah

Sometimes at a funeral home, we try to give reasons why this person died.

Especially when it has been a tragic death.

I sometimes find myself suggesting reasons why this might have happened, why it might be better this way, etc. I shouldn't do that.

I am not the Messiah. I am, like John the Baptist, here to help put people in touch with the Messiah. So I should simply feel the same sadness and confusion that they feel – and put them in touch with the Messiah, who can help them.

I am a minister, not the Messiah.

Sometimes when I pray, I try to be sure to include everyone in my prayer. I do this sincerely because I care about them and I want to help. So my prayer sometimes gets busy and cluttered because I'm trying to remember to mention all the intentions and all the people.

It is as though God wouldn't be able to handle this if I didn't take care of it. I have all these people depending on me (like the Messiah), and I work very hard to include them in my prayer.

I should realize that I am not the Messiah.

I do a little bit and I leave a lot in the true Messiah's hands.

Third Sunday of Advent/B cycle.

Only a day

I've been a priest for more than 37 years, and I've seen a lot of people die.

Whether they die as an old person or young or in-between, when you're with them when they're dying, they think of their past life as "only a day."

All of the past is hardly anything.

Everything is "right now."

They're dying, and they're going to the Lord.

They want to go to the Lord, saying, "I'm not perfect, but I tried to be truthful, and I tried to be true to you, and I tried to live goodness."

That is what means everything, and that is what brings a deep down happiness and peace not only when we're dying but every day along the way.

Our life is really "only a day."

Sixth Sunday in Ordinary Time/C cycle; February 11, 2001.

Come the kingdom

I have some grandnieces and grandnephews – two years old, a year-and-a-half.

When we get together, it's fun to watch the way little people act when they see somebody their own size whom they didn't know before.

They kind of stare at them and then they walk right up to them and look at them. And you know what they do sometimes? They push them because they don't yet know how to treat other people.

Now, on the other hand, if someone showed them a stuffed animal, they'd smile and go up and hug it.

It's interesting. They would treat a thing, a stuffed animal, better than they treat other little people. But they're little. They don't know yet. They've got to learn, and that's why we train them.

This is what struck me.

Sometimes people my age treat things better than people.

For example, our cars. Sometimes we treat our cars better than we treat some people. I know – I take care of my car. When it's cold, we want our car to be inside.

And sometimes we don't worry about people who sleep outside.

I listen to my car, listen for noises.

A lot of people I don't listen to.

Or our lawns. Sometimes we take care of our lawn better than we take care of other people.

I think of how important it is for me to remember that I'm grown up now. I should know better than small children. I should make sure I take care of people at least as well as I take care of things.

When I die and come to God, the only thing that will matter is the way I treated other people.

Twenty-second Sunday in Ordinary Time/C cycle; Lk 14:1, 7-14; Televised Mass for Shut-ins; August 30, 1998.

Good time to die

When I was in grade school, I used to think that the perfect time to die would be a Saturday.

It would be right after you went to confession, then said the Prayer before the Crucifix, and got the plenary indulgence. Then you walk out the church door, and get hit by a car.

I was thinking in terms of not having sins on your soul, but when Jesus talked about being ready to die, he talked in positive terms – about doing the things you were made to do. It's not a question of preparing for death by making sure there is no stain on our soul – we are a sinful, stained people. Rather, it is a question of living a life that involves the kinds of actions that God made us to perform.

That is how we become the persons we were made to be.

When would be a good time to die?

Well, I guess I would like to say when I died, that sometime within the last week I had given something away. That seems to be one of the things we were made to do, and I'd like to have been doing it when I died.

I would like to have spent a little time with someone who was lonely – maybe taken some extra time over coffee when I knew it would mean something to them. Jesus talked about things like that.

I sure would like to have had a smile on my face a lot, because Jesus called his disciples to be joyful.

I sure would want to have prayed and thought great thoughts.

I'd like to have been reading a good book, so that I was developing the gifts God gave me.

I'd like to have done something in the way of exercise, again to be developing God's gifts.

I would like to have forgiven someone . . . what I would not want would be to have resentment and anger at someone seething within me. That would be like dying with a whole basement full of stolen property.

Tuesday, twenty-ninth week of the year; Lk 12:35-38.

Why does God allow . . .

*I*n my 33 years as a priest, sometimes people expect me to be able to give answers to the great questions of "Why this? Why suffering?"

I can't.

There are times when all you can say is, "God is God, wider than ever I could understand. And God loves us and I don't know how it all works out. But God is God and I'm not."

I just want to assure myself and everyone that God is Emmanuel – God with us . . . and God is going to work it all out.

Third Sunday of Advent/A cycle; Jn 1:6-8; ordination of Steve Gavit to the transitional diaconate; St. John the Baptist Parish in Carrollton; December 15, 1996.

Exit interview

*O*rganizations sometimes do an exit interview with an employee who is leaving.

They ask how they found the working conditions there, what suggestions, they would have to make, and so forth.

I would like to do an "exit interview" with people on their deathbed. I would like to ask them to look back on the parish where they were a member and describe the things that they found helpful there in trying to make sense out of their life and in trying to live up to the Gospel.

It would be interesting to hear what they described.

Twenty-sixth Sunday in Ordinary Time/B cycle; Mk 9:38-43, 45, 47-48; St. James Parish in Bay City; commissioning of lay ministers.

To let go and die

I went to Mexico City to try to improve my Spanish. Arrangements were made so I would stay two weeks in a poor parish in a poor part of Mexico City, with a pastor who didn't speak any English. That's how I was going to improve my Spanish.

All the arrangements were made through somebody else who knew this person. I arrived in Mexico City and I never did get the name or address or anything because this priest was going to be there to meet me.

As I found out later, he thought I was coming the next day.

So I arrived, not any good in Spanish, and I'm standing there with all the arrivals, looking for someone to come up to me, and nobody came up.

Finally I wrote down on a piece of paper, "Untener," and I held it up.

After about three hours, some airport personnel came over and said, "Are you all right?"

I tried to explain to them what had happened. Well, it was a very big and busy airport. It was a frightening experience. There I was. I didn't know what to do. But I managed to reach somebody back in Saginaw who reached somebody who had made the arrangements, who then was able to call the person and tell them that they had the wrong date.

And I was helped. You can imagine how wonderful it was to see a friendly face appear with a smile.

For me, that's also an image of dying, because one could imagine dying and not seeing any friendly face. That gap. You've never been there before. You don't know what to do, where to go, and you don't see a friendly face.

The difference between that terrible experience and dying is seeing friendly faces, especially the Lord's friendly face. He says, "Why did you doubt? Why would you ever worry? We're close, and death could never break that friendship."

It takes great trust to let go and die. They say that death is always a conscious act, when the familiar and friendly hand of the Lord reaches out and he says, "Welcome home."

Memorial Mass for Joe Glaser; Mt 14:22-33; June 7, 2003.